How to be a "HIP" College Campus

How to be a "HIP" College Campus

Maximizing Learning in Undergraduate Education

Satu Rogers and Jeffery Galle

ROWMAN & LITTLEFIELD
Lanham • Boulder • New York • London

Published by Rowman & Littlefield
A wholly owned subsidiary of The Rowman & Littlefield Publishing Group, Inc.
4501 Forbes Boulevard, Suite 200, Lanham, Maryland 20706
www.rowman.com

Unit A, Whitacre Mews, 26-34 Stannary Street, London SE11 4AB

British Library Cataloguing in Publication Information Available

Library of Congress Cataloging-in-Publication Data Available

ISBN 978-1-4758-1901-4 (cloth : alk. paper)
ISBN 978-1-4758-1902-1 (pbk. : alk. paper)
ISBN 978-1-4758-1903-8 (electronic)

∞ ™ The paper used in this publication meets the minimum requirements of American National Standard for Information Sciences Permanence of Paper for Printed Library Materials, ANSI/NISO Z39.48-1992.

Printed in the United States of America

Contents

Acknowledgments

We would like to thank all the current and former faculty, students, staff, and administrators at Oxford College of Emory University who gave us their time to share their views, experiences, and insights that produced the material for this book. Most of the faculty and staff also reviewed the transcripts/notes we had taken during the interviews and sent us their approval and/or corrections. In their busy schedules, that was a lot to ask. As one faculty member pointed out, implementing high-impact practices takes more time than traditional instruction, and we know that none of the faculty have an excess of time.

We are also grateful to Stephen Bowen, Dean of Oxford College, for his support and editorial help in this project, as well as Cathy Wooten for feedback, editing, and suggestions. A special thanks to Dr. Shouping Hu of Florida State University, as well as the colleagues around the country who kindly commented on the book in the pages that follow and on the back cover. Finally, personal thanks to our spouses Hagen Rogers and Jo Galle for feedback on ideas and parts of the text, and supporting us throughout this three-year journey.

Satu Rogers, Greenville, SC
Jeff Galle, Atlanta, GA
February 8, 2015

Foreword

Making College Impactful

Higher education in the United States is at a delicate crossroads. College tuition continues to increase while the evidence on how much students learn from college points in an unfavorable direction. Colleges and universities undoubtedly need to do a better job in educating students.

Fortunately, decades of research on college students have resulted in the identification of some good practices that colleges and universities can adopt to promote student learning and personal development. The consistent research findings resulted in George Kuh terming these good practices "high-impact educational practices," now widely known as HIPs. HIPs encourage students to interact with faculty and peers in substantive ways and to devote considerable time and effort to educationally purposeful activities. Examples of HIPs include learning communities, undergraduate research, study abroad, and service learning.

The knowledge base for HIPs is strong, with the support of decades of work by higher-education scholars such as Astin, Chickering, Pascarella, Terenzini, and Kuh. Recent large-scale national studies, including the National Survey of Student Engagement (NSSE) and the Wabash National Study of Liberal Arts Education, further solidify the credibility of HIPs as ways to improve the overall quality of undergraduate education. If higher-education professionals desire to make college impactful on students, then HIPs should be a vital component of such an effort.

Thanks to the extraordinary effort of the Association of American Colleges and Universities (AAC&U), HIPs have become standard in the parlance addressing the quality of undergraduate education. The next step is for colleges and universities to experiment and implement HIPs to revitalize college education and optimize learning for all students.

In this book, Rogers and Galle use their own college, Oxford College of Emory University, as a case study and provide a meaningful example of how a college can implement HIPs. They collected data from in-depth, one-on-one interviews with twenty-one full-time faculty members from a range of disciplines and five staff/administrators, as well as focus groups with twenty-nine juniors or seniors. In their study, Rogers and Galle describe the importance of high expectations, student–faculty interaction, collaborative learning and leadership development, service learning, undergraduate research, and meaningful student diversity experiences.

ix

In particular, their campus used HIPs as a guide, and now these practices have permeated the campus. The commitment to HIPs must be communicated among campus constituents (i.e., all students, faculty, and administrators) in order for desired outcomes to occur.

Oxford College of Emory University reflects the principle of HIPs. The institution is deliberately creating conditions and opportunities for students to have meaningful interactions with key constituents on campus while devoting time and effort to educationally purposeful activities both inside and outside of classroom. In implementing HIPs, an institution should consider the campus environment and characteristics of the students and emphasize the shared responsibilities among students, faculty, staff, and administrators in the pursuit of student success in college.

One key takeaway from the book is that HIPs can be successfully implemented in colleges to enhance student learning and success. All students can benefit from engaging in HIPs. It is time for higher-education professionals and students alike to get to work and maximize the impact of college on students' educational experiences and outcomes.

Shouping Hu, PhD
Louis W. and Elizabeth N. Bender Endowed Professor
Director, Center for Postsecondary Success
Florida State University
Tallahassee, Florida

Preface

What is a "hip" campus? It may be one on which new teaching methods and technology are utilized, where students live in completely new kinds of dorms, or where there is very little structure (as some colleges already have) in the curriculum or degree plans. It may be one where teachers and students take on nontraditional roles or one where classes introduce innovative topics through lectures by famous persons in the industry.

It may be all of these, but in this book, we define it as a campus that uses high-impact educational practices (HIPs) extensively, both in and outside the classroom. These are practices that are known to have a high impact on students—for example, on cognitive and/or affective abilities. We discuss seven of these practices: (1) high expectations, (2) close and frequent student–faculty interaction, (3) effective teaching strategies ("good teaching"), (4) undergraduate research, (5) collaborative learning, (6) service learning, and (7) diversity (interactions). These are practices in which we believe our study campus to be particularly strong and there-fore offer insights for others.

This campus is Oxford College of Emory University, located thirty-eight miles from Emory's main campus in Atlanta. With a total of nine-hundred-plus students, it offers a liberal arts intensive curriculum for the first two years of a baccalaureate degree. After their sophomore year, students complete their junior and senior years on the main Emory cam-pus. Because of its focus on teaching, the first two years of college, the liberal arts, and general education, as well as its small size, Oxford Col-lege serves as a laboratory of teaching and learning.

Why is this important? For one, the freshman and sophomore years form a crucial period in young people's lives in that they are a transition-al period between the teenage years and young adulthood, and life at home and life in the "real world." Therefore they create a great opportu-nity for learning. In fact, Pascarella and Terenzini (1991)[1] find that much of critical-thinking skills develop during this time. In this book we show what can happen when HIPs are utilized in high frequency across cam-pus *during the first two years of a baccalaureate degree.*

HIPS AND WHY THEY MATTER

HIPs are practices, strategies, and pedagogical approaches used, qualities promoted, and experiences facilitated both in and outside of the classroom, especially in undergraduate education. They include such things as writing-intensive courses, internships, high levels of student–faculty interaction, and diversity experiences. As such, many of them represent or facilitate active and applied learning.

HIPs have been part of the higher education vocabulary especially since the 2008 publication of George Kuh's *High-impact educational practices*, and the use of the term by researchers in the Wabash National Study of Liberal Arts Education (2006–2012). Yet another, earlier, source of effective practices is Chickering and Gamson's (1987) "Seven principles for good practice in undergraduate education"—often quoted in faculty conversations. While Chickering and Gamson talk of principles, these principles overlap with, and are interchangeably called, good *practices*.

In his work, in conjunction with the Association of American Colleges and Universities, Kuh included ten different practices as HIPs. Of these, this study addresses four: undergraduate research, collaborative assignments, service learning/community-based learning, and diversity.[2] The other three HIPs that we discuss—high expectations, quality student–faculty interaction, and effective teaching strategies—originate in Gamson and Chickering's (1987) list and the Wabash National Study (2006–2012).

Why study the HIPs? Kuh has demonstrated that the use of HIPs promotes student learning. He analyzed two areas of the National Survey of Student Engagement (NSSE)—self-reported participation in various HIPs while in college and self-reported progress in select skills and dispositions during this time—and students' grades. He found that HIPs help improve the academic success of, particularly, "students from underserved populations"—specifically African Americans, Latino/a students, and those with lower ACT scores (McNair & Arbertine, 2012, p. 4, citing Kuh, 2008).

The biggest improvement according to his research was on black students' grades (Finley, 2012). Kuh also found a positive effect on first-to-second-year retention: especially Hispanic students returned to campus in greater numbers after the first year if they had participated in HIPs (ibid). With the share of students from minority groups increasing on campuses, we can expect HIPs to be increasingly relevant in the education of future students.

Shortly thereafter, in 2009, NSSE researchers conducted a study using National Survey data on four areas of perceived learning: a measure called deep learning, gains students felt they had made in general education, gains in personal and social development, and gains in practical competence. Their study of thirty-nine campuses in three states found that "[n]early every HIP examined [was] associated with significant gains" in these areas (Finley, 2011, p. 30).

They also found that some HIPs are more effective than others: of students' participation in the following six areas—learning communities (first year), service learning (both first and senior year), study abroad (senior year), student–faculty research (senior year), internships (senior year), and senior culminating experience—service learning was most clearly linked to high gains in the above outcomes. In Finley's words, "service learning experiences demonstrated the greatest impact on each of the four outcomes measured, regardless of whether the student was in the first or senior year" (ibid, p. 30).

While service learning is just one of the HIPs, its benefits are worth reviewing as it entails several characteristics common to HIPs: active and applied learning; a context of diverse individuals; students' responsibility for their own learning; and an emphasis on student roles that go beyond the campus, including citizenship and membership in one's community. It connects theory to practice (O'Grady, 2000). Its benefits include an increase in empathy toward others (Bok, 2006), "a sense of caring" (O'Grady, 2000, p. 8), self-esteem, changed social attitudes (ibid, citing Miller, 1994[3]), and leadership skills (Sax & Astin, 1998,[4] cited in Bok, 2006).

There is also extensive research about the connection of service learning/volunteering to the development of citizenship attitudes and social action orientation. This means students develop an understanding of social responsibility (O'Grady, 2000), conviction that students can change society, and commitment to "personally [a]ffecting social change" (Sax & Astin, 1998,[5] cited in Bok, 2006, p. 180). Summarizing several studies, Bok states that "community service programs have a positive effect on students' willingness to vote or work to improve their communities following graduation" (2006, p. 61).

Such benefits, especially at a time of declining citizen participation in the United States (as chapter 5 will show) as well as attacks against liberal arts education, point to the potential of HIPs in invigorating general and liberal education, enhancing student skills, and increasing students' campus and community engagement, including following graduation.

OUR CONTRIBUTION

It should be emphasized that while this study addresses benefits of HIPs, it is *not* an attempt to empirically measure the impact of, or assess, HIPs. Nor does it try to identify the exact mechanism via which these practices benefit students. Other researcher-practitioners have started to respond to the assessment call (see, for example, Finley & McNair, 2013). They have also sought to understand the extent to which students have equal access to these practices (ibid).

Rather, analyzing dozens of faculty, student (and staff) interviews, this book offers a narrative and practical insights about how HIPs work from multiple perspectives: those of faculty as well as students (and to a much lesser extent, staff and members of university administration). It makes three contributions to the work on HIPs.

First, it seeks to identify what kind of *institutional support and structure* a campus needs to have to enable the development of high-quality HIPs. To our knowledge, this enabling institutional framework for HIPs has not been discussed in other work. We draw our data from one campus that utilizes HIPs heavily. As the dean of this campus says, "Our institution is optimally organized to encourage and allow faculty to make use of HIPs in their teaching." Below, and to an extent in each chapter, we discuss how that is the case.

The second contribution is based on the kind of context in which HIPs are implemented: *early in the students' collegiate careers, and in a very diverse student population*. Both are more or less missed opportunities in scholarly research: HIPs are usually primarily thought of as having the most importance for the *last* two years of college. Also, to our knowledge they have not been specifically considered in a diverse college environment. Oxford College's program for the first two years of college takes place on an ethnically/racially diverse campus and with a high share of international students.

Third, while HIPs have received a great deal of attention since 2008, what is still needed is "developing more faculty capacity" in HIPs; it is "key to future success" (McNair & Albertine, 2012, p. 4). McNair and Albertine capture our thoughts: "Our campus colleagues tell us that we no longer have to convince them of the value of HIPs. They are asking us to focus instead on *practical means and methods to engage faculty with implementing HIPs in appropriate ways*" (ibid, p. 4, emphasis added).

To identify a repertoire of ways that faculty can effectively implement HIPs, we ask: What are effective strategies to employ HIPs? What do creative assignments based on active learning look like, and how can faculty steer students through them? What does a college need to take into account when wanting to help students interact with diverse others? What does teaching the whole student mean? We answer these and many other similar questions. Faculty strategies in a particular HIP is the theme that every chapter addresses.

THE CONTEXT: OXFORD COLLEGE OF EMORY UNIVERSITY

For a review of pedagogies and campus practices to make sense, we first need to know that they work. Therefore, the section below briefly reviews the extent to which students are successful on the study campus. Then, it describes the supportive campus environment and culture that enable this institution's faculty to utilize HIPs widely. The section concludes by describing the level of student diversity on campus.

Student Success

One indication of student success is student desire to continue their studies after the first year. At Oxford College of Emory University, the average first-to-second-year retention rate for five recent consecutive cohorts of incoming students (2008–2012) is 91 percent. This is quite high in an environment in which on average only 39 percent of this school's entering students during the above time period ranked this campus their first choice among colleges.[6] At peer institutions, on average 62 percent of entering students considered their campus their first choice among colleges.[7] Students' lower desire to attend Oxford means Oxford faces a greater challenge in ensuring that students persist and return for the second year.

Another indication of student success is graduation rate. At Oxford, six-year graduation rates are higher than those predicted by its student characteristics, when using a "predicted graduation rate calculator" created by the Higher Education Research Institute.

This calculator predicts graduation rates based on how large a share of students in the United States graduated in relation to these students' SAT scores, high-school GPAs, ethnicity, and sex. Specifically, in a group of forty-one private liberal-arts institutions similar to Oxford,[8] Oxford's over performance—that is, graduation rate above the predicted rate—in the 2004 incoming freshman cohort was the sixth highest. This means its graduation rate was 4.3 percentage points above the prediction.

Third, student interest in and graduation from science programs in particular can be considered another indicator of success. At Oxford, about 40 percent of incoming students typically express interest in science, technology, engineering, and math (STEM) degrees. Typically, this has been a higher share than at other institutions (see Figure 0.1.).

What is important is that of the 40 percent of Oxford students who express interest in STEM fields at the beginning of their college careers, a higher share than of students at other institutions (nationwide, on average) also *graduate* with a degree in STEM (see Figure 0.2.). That is, students who express initial interest in STEM majors *continue on to graduate in STEM disciplines at higher rates at Oxford than students nation-wide do*. In particular, as Figure 0.2. shows, Latino and African American student persistence in STEM fields is noticeably elevated when compared to national averages.

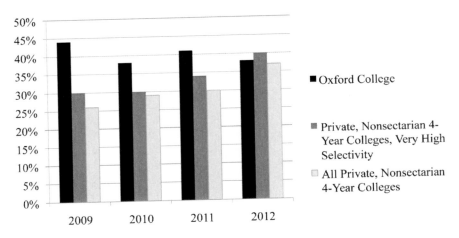

Figure 0.1. STEM as Students' "Probable Major" Upon Entering College, 2009–12. Source: CIRP Freshman Survey, Higher Education Research Institute (HERI), University of California, Los Angeles.

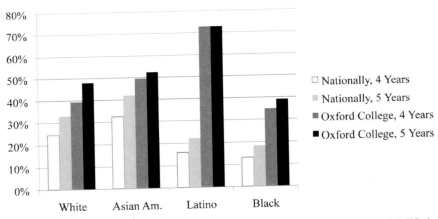

Figure 0.2. Percent of Those Initially Interested in STEM Graduating in STEM, 4- and 5-year Graduation Rates, 2003–05 Entering Students. Note: Oxford data refer to students among the 2003–05 entering cohorts indicating interest in STEM in the "Probable Major" question on the CIRP Freshman Survey (N=White, 140, Asian Am., 107, Latino, 11, and Black, 46), while the national data refer to the 2004 entering cohort ("Degrees of Success: Bachelor's Degree Completion Rates among Initial STEM Mayors," HERI Research Brief, Jan. 2010, Figure 2).

Fourth, students at the study institution volunteer and engage in community service actively. While objective comparative data on participation in service-learning classes are not publicly available, it appears, based on student reports, that freshmen at the study institution take service-learning classes more, or at least as, frequently as do students at other institutions. That is, according to NSSE data, a noticeably higher share of freshmen at Oxford report having *often* or *very often* participated "in a community-based project (e.g., service learning) as part of a regular course," compared to students at other NSSE institutions on average.[9]

Also, while Bok (2006) reports (true, based on data in the mid-1990s) that "the percentage of students who participate 'frequently' in service activities during high school drops by more than half in college" (pp. 167-168, citing an article by Astin[10]), at Oxford College involvement in service stays at the same level, or even increases, by the end of the sophomore year. While half of Oxford's incoming students say they participated frequently in volunteer work during their last year in high school,[11] as many as 57 percent of graduating sophomores report having actively participated in volunteer service during *either or both* of their years at Oxford.[12]

Supportive Campus Environment and Culture

Teaching and Faculty at the Forefront

How is the study campus organized to support the utilization of HIPs? McNair and Albertine (2012) write, "The development and delivery of high-quality high-impact practices depends on both institutional support and faculty dedication" (p. 5). Kuh (2008) would add that the beneficial impact of these practices on students also depends on students being adequately exposed to them (more than once). While students only complete the first two years of their baccalaureate degree on the Oxford campus, the campus offers them multiple and repeated opportunities for engagement in HIPs during this time.

There are at least two significant reasons that this campus is fertile ground for HIPs. First, there is a focus on teaching, with teaching skills and experience being the most important criteria in faculty recruitment. In the words of a former Dean of Academic Affairs, the institution seeks faculty who "fit in a culture that really values teaching." Also, faculty tenure and promotion criteria highlight teaching success: while "traditional disciplinary scholarship is . . . valued, . . . the greater emphasis is on the candidate's professional life as a teacher" (Bowen, 1999, p. 5).

At Oxford, all faculty, even those with twenty to thirty years of experience, teach general education courses. The average class size across disciplines and class levels during the freshman and sophomore years is just twenty-one.[13] This is a small class size for general education courses. Boyer's (1987) study emphasizes both of these factors: "[O]ne important way to measure a college's commitment to undergraduate education is to look at class size in general education. Do these courses enroll hundreds of students? Are they taught by senior professors?" (p. 145).

Second, "inquiry," or the pedagogical approach and defining feature of Oxford's educational program adopted relatively recently by the faculty encourages the use of HIPs. In 2008–2014, faculty and the administration developed and implemented an inquiry-driven approach to general education—which is now at the core of the institution's "liberal arts intensive" education.

While inquiry has long been practiced extensively in courses at this institution, it is now formalized, with students required to take at least three inquiry classes in different disciplines during their two years on campus. These disciplines must represent any two of the five different academic areas. Adopting this framework has resulted in an ever-increasing emphasis on engaged, student-centered and student-initiated learning, a key ingredient in several HIPs (see chapter 3).

Institutional emphasis on teaching and the inquiry approach results in other campus characteristics that help promote an extensive use of HIPs. For example, Oxford faculty members are encouraged to develop their courses and find new ways to express their dedication to teaching. In our interviews, faculty members shared their appreciation that an emphasis on teaching means they have "freedom to explore new teaching strategies," as a physics professor said.

This professor added, echoing the sentiments of others, "I don't feel the kind of pressure to work on improving my student evaluations that would not enable me to try new things." According to her, there is a spirit of collaboration among faculty, not competition, and the administration encourages experimenting with new techniques as well. Comments by several faculty members suggest that this campus possesses "faculty reward structures that support innovation in the classroom, including the use of technology to facilitate collaboration," which McNair and Albertine (2012) list as one of four conditions that help faculty develop and utilize HIPs successfully (p. 5).

Institutional emphasis on teaching also means, as implied, that the institution recognizes the importance of supporting faculty collaboration. Several faculty members pointed out how much they have learned from each other. Collaboration is an integral part of the faculty culture. At the center of it are conversations about pedagogy, a topic that at many other institutions "most professors would prefer to keep to themselves," since pedagogy concerns "the touchier question of how to teach one's courses" (Bok, 2006, p. 48).

The above physics professor continued to emphasize the interdisciplinary nature of faculty conversations on campus: "I think all disciplines can learn a lot from each other. . . . I try to incorporate things from all disciplines and all instructors." She thinks she would not be as good a teacher nor physicist if she only interacted with scientists. A chemistry professor agreed, saying she herself is "highly influenced by other faculty," and continued to characterize the institution "like a crucible" for such interactions and faculty mentoring.

Such features are not unrelated to an effective use of HIPs, but rather central. One could say they are prerequisites for them. If knowledge and experiences are not shared among faculty, insights cannot spread. But there is a role that the administration, too, plays in fostering such culture. An interviewed psychology professor stressed that an institution needs to ensure that faculty members have adequate time to interact with each other. Utilizing HIPs takes more time and effort to master than traditional, instructor-centered lecturing.

He added, "If the faculty are happy and engaged, the high-impact practices will come out. If not, faculty will go back to lectures. The desire to take risks comes from a feeling of safety. The more stressed you are, the more you are going to go back to what you know and what is 'safe.'"

Students at the Forefront

When faculty members have the freedom to explore and learn from each other, students are likely to benefit. Students also benefit when faculty are *expected* to spend time supporting students, as they are at the study institution. Faculty interaction with students outside of classes is valued. Most faculty, staff, and campus leaders take pride in being active in the "community." In our interviews, students attested to this, with the following comment from an upperclassman representing the experiences of many: "I can't even count the times I talked with [the Dean of Oxford College] or [the Dean for Campus Life], or visited their home."

Supportive campus environment also means there is close cooperation between faculty and staff, and *staff* support to students. At Oxford, faculty members generally feel that there is adequate staff support for their classes. Compared to her experience at other institutions, a physical education professor believes that her institution's faculty and staff "interact with each other more honestly and comfortably." An English professor gives an example: "Especially the library and IT services consider themselves partners in teaching. This helps faculty be creative and stay enthusiastic."

Fluid Boundary between Academics and Extracurricular Life

For students to have frequent exposure to HIPs requires that HIPs permeate students' educational experience. The study institution seeks to provide HIPs that integrate and incorporate students' academic and extracurricular lives, so that "academic learning" is facilitated in both contexts. The review of studies by Pascarella and Terenzini (1991) attests to the benefits of such integration: "[T]he more complete the integration between a student's academic life and social life during college, the greater the likelihood of his or her general cognitive and intellectual growth" (p. 159).

Campus Size

A final characteristic of a campus environment that is conducive to an effective use of HIPs that we highlight refers to the size of the student body and campus. Our study campus and its student body are both small (less than one thousand students). Students, faculty, staff, and administrators run into each other frequently—on the quad, at Lil's (campus cafeteria), and events such as theater performances and lectures. According to Pascarella and Terenzini (1991), small campus size promotes positive student outcomes indirectly "through the kinds of interpersonal relations and experiences it promotes or discourages" (p. 654). In the words of an English professor at Oxford, on a small campus, "students have the opportunity to be stars and to stand out."

This professor adds, "There is less hierarchy and bureaucracy. Students get the opportunity to be important in some parts of life—for example, student organizations and service learning. They have more opportunities to grow academically and to present themselves. They get to practice leadership and get feedback in that." Of course, student-centered HIPs are also easier to implement in small classrooms than in large lecture halls.

Student Diversity

The fact that this campus's educational program takes place in an ethnically/racially diverse environment and with a high share of international students is a central feature of the context. To begin with, there is a high level of structural diversity. While the college has had a high share of nonwhite domestic students for a long time, by 2013 this share had increased to about half of the student body. Also, the overall "minority" student population has expanded with the recent increase in the international student population (see data for 2001–2013 in Figure 0.3.). Among the nonwhite domestic students, Asian Americans make up the largest group.

Figure 0.3. shows that the jump in international student population occurred in 2010. Before then, non-US citizens were not widely represented on campus. That year, the share of international students in the freshman class was 22 percent, which has since then been followed by intentional balancing of international student numbers in the student population as a whole. In 2013, 17 percent of incoming freshmen were in the United States on F-1 (or other) nonimmigrant visas.

These developments mean that the white domestic student population has shrunk by 20 percentage points overall, from 54 percent of the freshman class in 2001 to 34 percent in 2013. We can therefore say that students who identify themselves as Caucasian are a minority on this

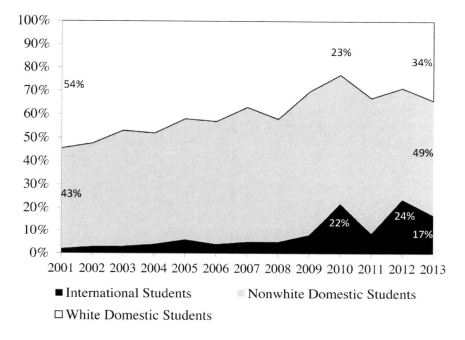

■ International Students   ▨ Nonwhite Domestic Students

□ White Domestic Students

Figure 0.3. Ethnic Diversity and Share of International Students in the Freshman Class, Oxford College, Fall 2001–13. Source: Emory University Registrar's Date of Record data.

campus. "This mix is unusual for a small college located in the South," says the Dean for Campus Life (Moon, 2009, p. 25).

Along with the change in ethnic/racial composition of the student body, there has been a change in the religious landscape, with an increase in the share of students professing no religion at all and a concurrent decrease in the share of Christian students (see Figure 0.4.).

Figure 0.4. shows that in 2001–2013, the biggest change in students' religious affiliation on this campus has been the three-fold increase in the share of students professing no religion at all, from 14 percent to 43 percent of the freshman class. In some years—2009, 2010, and 2012—this group has represented over half of the students. Beyond that, the combined share of students professing the four biggest non-Christian religions (Islam, Hinduism, Judaism, and Buddhism) has remained steady at about 15 percent.

In addition to the structural diversity, the campus has a strong emphasis on student interactions with diverse peers. When Oxford's freshmen participated in the Wabash National Study (2008–2009), clearly a higher share of students on this campus felt their school placed an em-

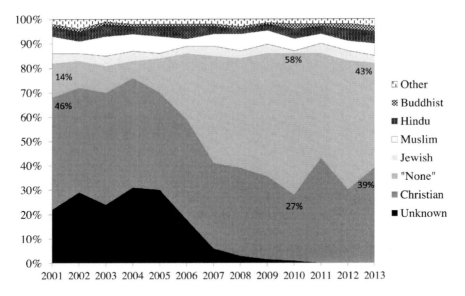

Figure 0.4.   Religious Affiliation in the Freshman Class, Oxford College, Fall 2001–13. Source: Emory University Registrar's Date of Record data.

phasis on diversity interactions, compared to students at other institutions.

Asked, "To what extent does your institution emphasize encouraging contact among students from different economic, social, and racial or ethnic backgrounds?," 45 percent of freshmen, compared to only 27 percent on other campuses, responded *very much*. In the questions asking students to report their frequency of interactions with diverse peers, Oxford students likewise reported significantly higher levels of such interactions compared to students in other schools on average.

Undoubtedly, part of the reason for frequent interactions is the fact that the campus is a close-knit community, in which it is hard for students to isolate, as Campus Life leadership describes the campus. The campus also practices inclusive diversity and mixed student governance, in which it is not uncommon for students of various races and religions to belong to clubs that are named after another race/religion. Another peculiarity is that survey data reveal that underrepresented minority students (i.e., blacks, Hispanics, and Native Americans) are actually more involved in active volunteering on this campus than are other students.[14]

While the small size of the campus may make the implementation of HIPs easier, this does not mean that HIPs cannot be successfully implemented in larger universities. For example, many universities have created learning communities to provide smaller settings in which students, faculty, staff, and the community can interact and learn from each other in intentional and structured ways.

The key in being a "HIP" campus is that students get frequent exposure to *high-quality* HIPs in and outside the classroom. Throughout this study, it became evident that the approaches and strategies that faculty, staff, and campus leaders use, the expectations they set, and ways they interact with students have immense potential to positively impact students academically and psychologically.

NOTES

1. Cited in Bok (2006).
2. To the discussion on collaborative learning we add leadership development because we find that collaboration and leadership skills are intricately linked. We also widen the discussion on service learning and community-based learning to address teaching the "whole student," of which we consider service learning and community-based learning to be a part.
3. Miller, J. (1994). Linking traditional and service-learning courses: Outcome evaluations utilizing two pedagogically distinct models. *Michigan Journal of Community Service Learning, 1*(1), 29–36.
4. Sax, L. J. & Astin, A. W. (1998). Developing civic virtue among college students. In J. N. Gardner & G. Van der Veer (Eds.), *The senior year experience: Facilitating integration, reflection, closure and transition,* San Francisco, CA: Jossey-Bass, p. 133.
5. See previous note.
6. Many of them wanted to enroll on Emory's main campus instead.
7. In Fall 2008, these peers were the other thirty-three liberal arts institutions participating in the Wabash National Study. In 2009–2012, they were private/nonsectarian four-year colleges with "very high" selectivity as documented by the Cooperative Institutional Research Program (CIRP) Freshman Survey administered by the Higher Education Research Institute (HERI) of UCLA.
8. Higher Education Data Sharing (HEDS) consortium peer institutions.
9. NSSE 2008: 38 percent at study institution versus 14 percent at other National Survey institutions on average; NSSE 2012: 25 versus 15 percent. The actual course data from Oxford indicate that about 40 percent of students take a service-learning class during their freshman and/or sophomore year.
10. Astin, A. W. (1996). Involvement in learning revisited: Lessons we have learned. *Journal of College Student Development, 37,* pp. 123, 129.
11. Source: CIRP Freshman Survey (2009, 2010, and 2011).
12. 2013 Oxford College Graduation Survey.
13. Fall 2013. Following the Common Data Set definition, this excludes laboratories, independent study, directed readings (and all one-on-one courses), and classes that are not identified by a discipline, do not meet "in a classroom or a similar setting," and/or are not credit bearing.
14. Oxford College Graduation Survey.

Introduction

Of the high-impact practices (HIPs) promoted by Chickering and Gamson (1987), Kuh (2008), and Wabash National Study (2006–2012), this study discusses seven, as mentioned above, in seven separate chapters. It also addresses practices that are not found on these lists but that the interviewees emphasized as effective practices and experiences, and that, one can argue, are closely related to the established HIPs, including leadership-skill development and teaching the whole student. Other "established" HIPs outside the seven mentioned, such as writing-intensive courses, capstone experiences, and internships, are not covered.

The data source consists of in-depth, one-on-one interview material from twenty-one full-time faculty from a range of disciplines and from five staff/administrators (all on the study campus), as well as focus group data from twenty-nine students, enrolled as juniors or seniors at the time of interview. All the interviewed faculty had years—some, decades—of teaching experience. Faculty, staff, and administrators were interviewed in Fall 2012 and Spring 2013, and students in Spring 2013. All participants were recruited through a call for volunteers. This call was announced in an annual faculty retreat and via an email to hundreds of students majoring in various disciplines.

In the interviews, faculty were asked to describe their pedagogy, engagement with students, assignments, syllabi, feedback, and any other dimensions of their interaction with students that they felt enhanced student learning. In turn, students were asked to think back to their experience on campus and describe what helped them learn. They were asked to evaluate the academic rigor they faced, how their interaction with faculty affected their learning process, what they felt was most effective/challenging in their education, and so on. The interview transcripts were analyzed for lessons learned.

ORGANIZATION OF THE BOOK

Each thematic chapter begins with a short account of past studies on and experience by other campuses with the HIP in question. This is not a comprehensive review of research on the topic, nor a traditional literature review, whose goal is to identify competing explanations for hypotheses. *This study does not advance, in that it does not test, specific hypotheses.*

The task of the first part of each chapter is to place the practical examples that follow in the context of higher-education trends/development. The practical examples are about how faculty have most effectively implemented each practice, and how students have responded.

Neither is this a study of student outcomes, as emphasized earlier, although we do refer to learning outcomes. It is rather a review of inputs, suggesting that there is likely a link between the use of high-impact pedagogies and student success.

The chapters that follow are organized so that they build on each other. The first one, "High Expectations," is about a HIP without which none of the other practices really matter. It asks and answers how faculty can set high expectations for students in a way that inspires students to give their best performance yet does not overwhelm them. It lays the groundwork for discussing the rest of the HIPs.

In turn, because students are able to successfully meet high expectations only when they also receive adequate support, chapter 2, "Support through Interaction," discusses the importance of high-*quality* (and frequency of) student–faculty interaction and the various forms this interaction can take.

Next, due to its subject matter, chapter 3, "Effective Teaching Strategies," is the most comprehensive chapter in the book. While the bulk of the book is about effective teaching, this chapter deals specifically with pedagogies, strategies, and characteristics that make up (a) "good teaching"—a group of key ingredients of successful liberal arts education as defined by the researchers of the Wabash National Study (2006–2012)—and (b) three distinct strategies promoted by Chickering and Gamson (1987) among their "seven principles for good practice in undergraduate education."

The three strategies promoted by Chickering and Gamson are: using active learning techniques, giving prompt feedback, and respecting diverse ways of learning. In addition, chapter 3 discusses the importance of such issues as faculty's passion for teaching, creative assignments, students' emotional identification with the subject matter, clarification of students' biases, getting students out of the contexts to which they are accustomed, and embedding mistakes or errors into lectures by design.

Chapter 4, "The Undergraduate Research Experience," follows this by adding to the definition of good teaching research with students. Effective courses typically offer research opportunities for students. This chapter discusses the psychological importance of "respecting students' minds," something that a number of faculty saw as an important part of developing students' capabilities. This means viewing even freshmen and sophomores as mature and capable, entrusting them with challenging research assignments, sharing excitement about research with them, and viewing them as research partners.

Next, chapter 5, titled, "Collaborative Learning and Leadership Development," discusses a practice that in a way permeates (or can permeate) all others: collaborative learning. The chapter ties collaboration with leadership. While leadership development is usually not formally recognized as a HIP, it can be argued to be intertwined in effective collaboration. Here, leadership refers to working with a team and being able to operate effectively in groups with a sense of social responsibility. A "hip" campus seeks to develop leadership skills in *freshmen* giving them recognition and opportunities to lead.

Also related to collaboration and leadership, chapter 6, "Teaching the Whole Student: Taking Learning into the Realm of Experience," discusses teaching with the whole student in mind. As such, it addresses service- and community-based learning, a HIP that promotes students' capacity and likelihood of being active and informed citizens. Faculty stress the need to teach to the soul and spirit, not just the mind.

As the final chapter on an individual HIP, chapter 7, "Putting HIPs in Context: (Interactions with) Diversity," ties the preceding chapters together through the theme *diversity*, which is both a HIP and at the same time the context for all other HIPs. While interacting with diverse others is a skill campuses seek to promote, diversity is also a setting in which all of the above HIPs will increasingly take place as the shares of both minorities and international students increase. With high shares of non-white domestic students (in Fall 2012 and 2013 on average 45 percent of all freshmen) and students from other countries (20 percent non-US citizens), the study campus is well placed to test the functioning of the HIPs amidt this kind of a population.[1]

The last chapter, chapter 8 ("Summary and Conclusions"), summarizes the lessons learned and identifies implications for other institutions. It tackles the question to what extent lessons are exportable to other contexts. The chapter reiterates the importance of the early engagement of students that is so vital at the study campus. When relevant opportunities are offered to students early on, whether in academics or extracurricular life, and combined with high expectations of student responsibility and quality of student work, experience indicates that by and large, students take advantage of the opportunities, rise to the challenge, and benefit by maximizing their learning.

NOTE

1. The rest of the freshmen were white domestic students (31 percent) and those whose ethnicity was unknown (3 percent).

ONE

High Expectations

High expectations are a linchpin of good education. Without challenge, not much learning can occur. The interviewed faculty agreed that for expectations to be most effective, there needs to be a *shared commitment* to requiring much of students early on. This can mean high quality in completed assignments, large volume of reading/writing, and/or the development of such attributes as emotional maturity, discernment, or demonstrated growth in academic skills over time.

For example, a sociology professor defined expectations with reference to growth in students' ability to distinguish between what is important and what is not and understanding the central issues of their times. While not minimizing the comprehension of theory, his focus seems to be on helping students build perspective by enhancing their understanding of the context(s) in which they live and assuming an active role in the world.

"Perspective" also means that students need to realize how much they still have to learn. The professor explains: "Whatever discipline students study, they are surrounded by a world that is extraordinarily complex. Their surface understanding does not exhaust all there is to know, understand, or imagine about these disciplines. So part of what I do is fire students' imagination and understanding that they do not know everything there is to know."

The professor goes on to give an example of how superficial students' knowledge often is. His students easily know about the Monica Lewinsky affair of 1998—when the students were very young—"yet could not name a single piece of legislation moving through any legislative body anywhere in the world that will have an impact on any aspect of their well-being." The professor wants to demonstrate that issues like this one on Bill Clinton will go away. "I tell them that what is real is the quality of the air they breathe and their diet," he stresses. "I want to set the stage for people to grow in their intellectual and civic skills and be present in the issues that define their times."

This example reiterates that besides expecting and teaching purely academic skills, faculty can challenge students' assumptions, priorities, and the extent to which students care about current issues, the environment, and/or others. High expectations thus often call for self-examination by the students. If faculty challenge students in these ways, helping them go beyond the fleeting interests of the moment, they can facilitate significant learning for them. Students will engage with the course material on a deeper and more personal level, and the bar for performance is raised.

This chapter first outlines how various practitioners, analysts, and campuses have understood and applied this high-impact educational practice. It then reviews further examples about how faculty think about and set expectations for their students, and how students respond.

HIGH EXPECTATIONS IN HIGHER EDUCATION

According to one definition, academic challenge—another name for high expectations—is a "range of activities from time spent studying to the nature of intellectual and academic tasks students are expected to perform at high levels of accomplishment" (Kuh et al., 2005, p. 177). It thus pertains both to the quantity and quality of student work, in addition to the development of certain attributes and characteristics, as suggested above.

The quintessential importance of having high expectations is certainly not a new idea. In their oft-cited 1987 article in the *AAHE Bulletin*, Chickering and Gamson describe "communicates high expectations" as one of the fundamental principles for good practice in undergraduate education. Similarly, the Wabash National Study (2006–2012) identifies academic challenge and high expectations as one of four key predictors of student success in liberal arts education.

Yet low levels of expectation continue to characterize the education of many students in the twenty-first century, as Ozturk and Debelak document,[1] arguing that this is so *on all levels of education in the United States*. The result, as the authors show, is that academic performance of American students continues to fall behind international comparisons. And not only international comparisons but instructor complaints about student preparation suggest that students entering each level of education have not been required to perform at levels they should have been required to perform (ibid).

Past studies have established an empirical link between academic challenge and student success. For example, Schilling and Schilling (1999) outline: "[C]lassic studies in the psychology literature have found that merely stating an expectation results in enhanced performance, that higher expectations result in higher performance, and that persons with high expectations perform at a higher level than those with low expectations, even though their measured abilities are equal" (p. 5).

The authors go on to stress the importance of establishing high expectations in students' first semester of study, as "[s]tudents appear to determine in their first months on campus how much time they will devote to academic pursuits, and this pattern of time allocation is durable over the rest of their college experience. What is required of students in their first semester appears to play a strong role in shaping the time investments made in academic work by students in their last semester of their senior year" (ibid, p. 8). This suggests that faculty who teach freshmen play an especially important role in establishing expectations for college study.

Studies have also established links between challenge and specific learning outcomes. For example, by studying forty-nine institutions of higher education, researchers in the Wabash National Study (2006–2012) found that challenging students and requiring high levels of effort are connected to growth in such skills as critical thinking, moral reasoning, socially responsible leadership, and other liberal arts outcomes.

Using the Wabash National Study data, Mayhew et al. (2012) found that academic challenge has positive effects on moral reasoning *particularly among those students whose moral development is not yet "consolidated."* And in a very influential recent book, *Academically adrift* (2011), Arum and Roksa documented that challenge is often lacking in undergraduate education, with deleterious consequences.

In Arum and Roksa's study, only 42 percent of the 2,300 students who began as freshmen in 2005 in twenty-four colleges and universities across the country said they had had at least one class in the previous semester that required forty pages of reading per week and one class that required twenty pages of writing. When students are not required to do more than that, it may not be surprising that the documented learning across the study campuses was low: 36 percent of students showed *no* measurable improvement between the beginning of the freshman year and the end of their senior year in reading, analysis, reasoning, and writing skills.[2]

Not surprisingly, Arum and Roksa's findings support the importance of using educational practices that promote rigor—such as coursework requiring reading and writing at significant levels. If lack of academic rigor is at the center of the problem, as the authors' data demonstrate, then one obvious solution is the development of rigorous courses and higher faculty expectations for student learning.

However, expectations should not be equated with workload—despite the fact that adequate exposure to the material is certainly necessary. For example, Wiggins and McTighe (2005) caution teachers of the "twin sins" of course design, which consist of the "tyranny of coverage" (covering too much material at the expense of deep learning), and, on the other hand, having students engage in hands-on activities without critically thinking and evaluating those activities (cited in Gamer, 2013, pp. 1–2).

Beyond higher-education researchers, some institutions, recognizing the value of challenge/high expectations, have undertaken studies of this topic on their campuses. Many of these emphasize both quality (difficulty) and quantity (time on task) that are needed to improve student performance.

For example, in Indiana, the Taskforce on Academic Rigor at Ball State University (2013) issued a report emphasizing such things as an intellectually challenging and demanding environment, deep disciplinary knowledge, and an "engaged pursuit of a challenging and recognized educational goal" in the institution's quest for more rigor (p. 7). The latter could translate to faculty consciously setting and articulating goals for the specific skills, knowledge, and/or dispositions that they want their students to learn in their course, discipline, or the educational program in general.

In California, California State University at Chico has created university-level policy that describes and defines the level of importance the institution gives to academic challenge. Entitled unambiguously "Academic Rigor at California State University, Chico," the CSU-Chico statement comes in two parts—"Rigorous Teaching" and "Rigorous Learning"—with the first part including many of the good practices offered by Chickering and Gamson in the 1980s. The bulleted items in the second part underscore the need for ethics, respect of others, honesty, and integrity.

While such declarations emphasize the value given to academic challenge, changes within the academic culture and broader campus culture can only occur as faculty, students, and staff adopt and apply the values in concrete ways. There seems to be better documentation of the existence and development of these values on the level of individual classes for specific faculty, of which a few examples are outlined below.

FACULTY IMPLEMENTATION OF HIGH EXPECTATIONS AND STUDENT RESPONSE

Faculty interviews gave a clear indication of both the need for a shared commitment to requiring much of students and, on the other hand, the fact that expectations naturally manifest very differently and focus on different skills and areas depending on the discipline, class, and professor. Below are themes that arose both in faculty interviews about how faculty understand and "use" this HIP and how students respond when much is required of them.

Commitment to High Levels of Challenge Early On

Interviews with both faculty and students enrolled in junior and senior grades confirmed that an expectation of student success is powerful when there is a campus-wide commitment to it, starting from the early months of the freshman year. Then, students are less likely to question or complain about it—it is a shared norm. Also, faculty seemed to agree that a mere absence of upperclassmen on campus should not mean that faculty cannot expose students to challenge.

In a math professor's words, "Students are capable of being challenged much more than we think." Similar statements were expressed by faculty across disciplines. "You are doing them a disservice if you give them only easy things to do, undermining their intelligence," said a physics professor. "Giving them challenging assignments tells them, 'I know you can do this.'" She relates the ability to respond to challenge to stubbornness, as "stubbornness is an important part of science." So is a certain level of struggle, she continues. She shares with her students that "if they are not struggling, they are not learning."

Discipline-Specific Implementation

As suggested at the beginning of the chapter, high expectations can refer to a range of skills and qualities that faculty expect to see in students. When asked about the topic, a biology professor (biology professor #1) stressed that in her discipline, high expectations have to do with course content, level of understanding, research skills, scientific writing, and "thinking and working like a scientist." Students have to master the material and also solve problems and apply the knowledge. Another biology professor (biology professor #2) emphasized that to really understand scientific concepts, students need to know a certain level of detail, "despite the fact that science is not just a list of facts." This is in addition to them needing to have a depth of understanding and ability to synthesize information.

Sometimes—or perhaps often—faculty and students have different definitions for good performance. According to biology professor #2, students often expect that "if I know the facts, I will do well," though in reality, she continues, "to earn an 'A' in my class means students really master the information. Such a student knows the information at a much higher level than others."

She explains:

> We really want students to start working as if they were a researcher in the field. . . . You do not just go through a check list. You have to look at the data and think about it. . . . They have to decide which data should be presented, and which not; which should be condensed, which should be presented in a table versus a graph, and so on. . . . I always

have to tell them it is not about what I want, but about the level of excellence you see if you open up a scientific journal.

The professor explains that in her nonmajors' biology class, she expects students to write a scientific paper in the style that is expected for a published journal article. "I know students do not do that kind of lab work, but they have to learn the style and format of such a paper."

Increasing Amount of Independent Work

As implied above, one manifestation of high expectations is increasing amounts of independent work. A chemistry professor establishes her expectations for independent work right at the start of the semester, telling her students on the first day:

> I will ask you to do something you think you cannot do, but I will help you do it. During the last two weeks of the semester you will design your own procedure to extract caffeine from an energy drink. Every week when you come to lab I am not going to give you a procedure to follow. You will have to learn to do it yourself. The experiments will become more difficult as the semester progresses but you will be repeating the techniques over and over in different ways. At the end of the semester you will be ready.

Students' reaction to this is that "at first, they are absolutely terrified. But usually," the professor continues, "by about week five, they will see that they are understanding what they are doing. They will have started to learn to put the pieces together. By the end of the semester every one of them can carry it out."

To this professor, a very important element of challenge is that students are not asked to follow cookbook instructions. "They need to figure out the 'how' themselves."

Independence also has to do with what is done in class, and what is not. A professor of ancient languages requires his students to take responsibility for the basic work of language acquisition such as learning vocabulary and verb tenses on their own, devoting time in class to higher-order learning. He does not use class time for the vocabulary quizzes or grammar reviews students would have had in high school.

"That is something they should do in their dorm rooms," he stresses. "I tell students that this needs to become a habit like brushing your teeth, and that they need to take responsibility for it: no one needs to tell you to brush your teeth. You just do it." He argues that students should develop the same habit in their learning of languages. Learning vocabulary that does not require the professor's presence just prepares them for learning higher-order skills in class.

Other Manifestations of High Expectations

Other manifestations of high expectations include both broader and very specific examples. An example of the former, the sociology professor quoted at the beginning of the chapter talks about students' overall development and maturation. Working from the expectation that students can be "self-disciplined, that they want to take serious ideas seriously," he believes challenge permeates all that faculty do, including mentoring. It is a broader call than just testing students through exams in class; it involves how students can be "successful as adults."

But high expectations also manifest in class, on a more micro level. For example, a political science professor cultivates high expectations by "not allowing students to be silent and wearing me down." His emphasis is on learning in an active way.[3] And in humanities, an English professor lets his students know that "grammar and mechanics are things that I take very seriously." However, he does not leave it at that; he likes to always, "when I can, provide a historical perspective (to, for example, grammar and mechanics), so students see that there is a very long and rich perspective to university learning." This helps students put particular expectations into context and understand the reasons for the expectations.

Outside of class, in student life, high expectations manifest in holding students accountable to the mission, values, and/or goals of the club or organization to which they belong. Thus high expectations are not only the domain of academics; they can characterize cocurricular life as well.

Conveying of Expectations

How are expectations conveyed? The professor can do this through the syllabus, course material, lectures, and assignments. A professor of religion emphasizes the importance of a long and detailed syllabus: "We spend quite some time with it in class. I want my students to understand what they are signing up for." He also uses multiple texts and weekly reading responses, and stresses that it is important for assignments to steer away from regurgitation, instead requiring students to demonstrate how one reading is connected to another. A number of faculty also use weekly or daily quizzes to check completion of required readings.

Individual course design can reveal both a high level of challenge and the expectation of student success. In a sophomore course in pharmacology, a psychology professor hands out a picture of a pill to each student on the first day of class. He then announces that one major semester project will be the identification of the pill, followed by in-depth research on its benefits and dangers, culminating in a student presentation (frequently a PowerPoint and more often a video) that expresses students' knowledge in an accurate and often humorous way.

In place of a lecture for this part of the course, this professor developed a challenging assignment that calls for a great deal of student independent research and creativity. Students spend many days researching first and then creating the presentation that captures the usefulness of their pill. Hence, pedagogical innovation, combined with a challenging assignment (and course content as well) with a high expectation of student success lead to the kind of academic challenge that Chickering and Gamson and others describe.

Helping Students Face the Expectations

In the face of a great challenge, what are some ways students stay motivated—believing they are able to respond to the challenge and then meet the expectations? How can faculty make high expectations palatable? Students may have false ideas about their capabilities, in which case they need to be helped to see that they *can* meet the challenge.

The professor of ancient languages and classics quoted above describes a sample conversation from his writing intensive class:

> For example, when students who like football say they have never formulated the kinds of arguments necessary for scholarly work, I tell them, "Yes, you have. Think about the best quarterback in the NFL, for example. If you think it is Tom Brady, and someone says it is Peyton Manning, you will say, 'No it's not—and here's the evidence.' You tell them about statistics, and everything you know about what makes Tom Brady the best quarterback—you put together a very tight argument, an evidence-based argument."

In addition, several faculty emphasized that students proceeding through an assignment need guidance, or concrete scaffolding. This is something very active and takes a lot of time. For example, in a library workshop, biology professor #2 emphasizes: "The point is that we are not just sending students off without an idea of what the expectation is. It is very important to have them not to stay lost. Scaffolding includes preventing them from being completely lost." As part of this it may be helpful for faculty to think through students' likely path in configuring the assignment and their response.

She explains her strategy for guiding her nonmajor students in the professional paper she assigns them:

> How do I get them to really understand that they are capable of doing that? I have to do it in steps. . . . I have them read a paper that has a good bit of technical language, but deals with a topic that they might find interesting. One such paper was about cardiovascular health and exercise. Another one was about compounds found in food. Usually I pick something that is health related, so that they can identify with it. They have to write a response, in which I specifically ask them to pay attention to the format: what is included in each section, how the infor-

mation is presented, and so on. Even if they look at it first and think it looks like a bunch of technical jargon, I ask, "But what did you actually learn from it? You do not have to get caught up in the technical jargon."

Her guidance thus involves giving students specifics as to what to look for in the article so that they know exactly what is expected of them.

"Another thing," she continues, "is humor. I am kind of commiserating with them. I tell them, I am here for you—tell me how I can help with this challenge. I tell them I know it is hard. That is another part of the partnership I have with them. I think requiring a certain level of challenge really requires putting yourself in their place. We should think about what would help *me* if I was in their place."

Biology professor #1 agrees: it is important to be truthful with students about the challenge involved. But it is also important to "help them see the hidden reward." For example, doing an excellent job may help students gain access to medical school and ultimately succeed in their career. Discussing the positive consequences of high expectations and challenging courses or assignments can help students look beyond the immediate costs of the challenge, and find satisfaction in delayed gratification.

Costs of High Expectations

What *are* the costs of high expectations? They can include stress and inability to sleep, and can extend to social relationships. The Wabash National Study records that when students attempt to meet expectations both in the classroom, and—regarding level of involvement—in extracurricular life, they may have to pay a price in other areas. For example, it is not unrealistic to anticipate that increases nationally in student visits to college counseling centers due to mental health problems such as anxiety and depression are related to large workload and high expectations that students feel they cannot meet (American Psychological Association, 2011).

In requiring much of their students, the challenge for faculty is to know how to uphold the high expectations while also helping students believe that the expectation is achievable. Faculty awareness of where students are is key.

While more aspects of faculty support of students will be discussed in the next chapter, the following comment by biology professor #2 refers to the important role that faculty play through encouragement and scaffolding when expecting that students will meet their challenge successfully:

You always have to be very aware of what is happening to the students as they go through the experience. Which parts of the assignment are uncomfortable, and how can you help students to where you would really love for them to be? I have tried to observe these to know where I can provide more guidance. Providing the appropriate guidance is key. Otherwise you end up with a hostile attitude from the students. You need to encourage a positive attitude toward your assignments and goals.

Student Perspectives

Beyond faculty interviews, asking students about their learning, impressions of classes, and their sense of what works and what is less effective remains even today an often untapped way of assessing what goes on in the classroom. In reality, students can be very articulate about the "what" of their classes and intuitive about the "why" a particular activity is being used. Students were asked to describe their academic experience and recall specific assignments, activities, and professors who challenged them even from the first day of classes.

One student thought it is very helpful to be "pushed far, forced to engage in a certain type of academic language, and pushed to think of things in a very different way." Another student followed up, recounting a specific chemistry professor who "pushes you individually," continuing, "I wouldn't be doing as well as I'm doing if it wasn't for the way she pushed me." In turn, another student suggested that *not* being challenged reduces her motivation. She said she once took a class (on another campus) in which "I had to ask for permission to do the next step. I felt very childish. I didn't want to try it, because it wasn't challenging and I didn't have to do any thinking."

Several students recounted their experiences in math, perhaps not surprisingly. One student explained how in a pure math class students faced the challenge of "breaking complex processes down into simpler stages or steps." The student related how the requisite analysis translated well in later junior- and senior-level math classes. Another's recollection involved the metacognitive domain: "The very way we approached problems was challenged from the first day in calculus class. We had to think about what assumptions we used in approaching every problem."

Yet another student appreciated the fact that in linear algebra, "we had to teach the material to the other students. They asked us questions; we had to ask them questions." And further, in a literature course on the work of Virginia Woolf, two students explained, "We read and discussed not only Woolf's novels but also journals and other historical and archival texts. We used them to raise questions that scholars might raise, but we went on to develop answers to these questions ourselves."

These examples indicate that students generally appreciate being "pushed" as it enables them to achieve something they feel they otherwise would not achieve. One student summed it up: "I think that expectations make a really big difference. . . . We live up to the expectation."

She indicated it is especially refreshing when there is the "expectation to enjoy learning for learning's sake."

In summary, an examination of the student and faculty narratives leads to the identification of certain recurring and overlapping features of academic challenge and faculty expectations. Both faculty and students perceive the following as key characteristics of high expectations, with expectation of success:

a. Making the goals of courses far more ambitious than just learning content;
b. Compelling students to take responsibility for the basic learning so that the professor can concentrate on the higher order goals;
c. Compelling the students to play an active role in pursuit of those higher learning goals with emphasis on reflection/metacognition; and
d. Providing scaffolding to facilitate the achievement of expectations.

Realizing these is best possible in small classes—and on a smaller campus—in which the faculty can more easily monitor the progress of individual students.

Also emerging from the faculty interviews and student focus groups is the shared sense among both groups of what a sound academic challenge is *not*: simply creating more assignments, extending study hours, keeping students busy, memorizing facts, covering every idea in the textbook. They do not necessarily lead to deeper learning, improved application of ideas in new contexts, or improved skills.

Students acknowledged the heavy workload that high expectations caused and the many late nights juggling student leadership responsibilities and academic assignments, but what they focused on were the ways in which faculty drew them out, challenged them in a variety of ways, and rewarded creativity and intelligence with opportunities for research and recognition. Faculty also emphasized the idea of working alongside their students, providing them with a course design that progressively staged students' independent inquiry.

Notwithstanding the amount of reading and the number of assignments included in course syllabi, neither group spent much time describing (even though it is also important) how many books they read each semester or how many writing assignments the course required. Students readily acknowledged, "Of course there was a lot of reading and writing," but as juniors and seniors, they recognized the value of the challenge, and what they learned from it.

NOTES

1. While Ozturk and Debelak's article is not dated, it is clear from their bibliography that the article was not written before summer 2005.

2. Results come from the Collegiate Learning Assessment (CLA) exam.

3. See chapter 3 for more on this topic.

TWO

Support through Interaction

The previous chapter examined the first half of a very powerful equation—high expectations combined with academic challenge. Faculty who communicate high expectations of student performance when their courses possess considerable rigor invite industriousness and creativity by asking students to engage deeply in the material at hand. In classes such as these, students can perceive the seriousness with which faculty approach complex materials. It is important for faculty in such classes to repeatedly send the message that students can succeed. "You *can* do this," should be at the heart of the communication with students in a variety of contexts.

High-quality interactions with faculty and campus support staff—the second part of the powerful equation—are necessary for most students to believe that they can successfully respond to faculty's calls for excellence. Such interactions, centered in the classroom and the lab where so much of importance occurs, help students feel supported in their attempts to fulfill requirements and excel. Extending from class time to office conversations, and further to a wide array of other contexts, faculty and staff need to engage students by relating to them as individuals, not merely as "brains on a stick," which refers to Uhl's (2011) name for an outmoded view (p. 16).

Possible scenarios include the following. In the lab for biology class Cell Biology and Genetics, a professor works side by side with her first-year students. Ideally, there is a minimal use of teaching assistants; faculty teach their own labs. Not to abandon the questions and visits of other students, the professor places a note on her office door: "You can find me in the lab."

In another professor's Political Science 100—National Politics in the United States—students find the professor offering out-of-class study sessions early in the morning. Nearly every student attends the early morning preclass sessions, because the professor makes himself available for questions of any sort on any part of the material at hand.

Finally, an English professor hosts dinners at her home several times a semester for students in her American Literature class, and at these dinners students talk about their academic experiences at the college. The dinners offer students the opportunity to talk about any particular book selection that they have been reading and writing about, but more importantly, by opening her home to her students, the professor provides a good venue for discussion of wider ranging topics and a little home cooking away from home.

From classroom/lab context, to extra class meetings, to off-campus dinners, the faculty who teach such courses are finding different ways to send the message "You can do this," to their students. These three examples—one from the physical sciences, one from the social sciences, and one from the humanities—illustrate several key elements. No single academic area or specific discipline has exclusive hold on the contexts in which meaningful interactions can occur.

Second, there is no single way in which faculty can establish interactions with students that lead to intellectual anticipation and personal excitement for the students. In the office, the lab, the classroom, and farther in a club setting, a student activity, or in the faculty's home, all of these and more provide the venue within which high-quality and positive interactions can occur. And third, what occurs within each context is quite meaningful for the students, both in those cases where the academic content is explicitly the focus and in those where discussion is more personal. This chapter explores ways in which faculty (and staff) can interact with students to support student learning, in ways that are rewarding to all parties.

PAST STUDIES ON STUDENT–FACULTY INTERACTION

Not surprisingly, the findings from a number of studies underscore the importance of interactions between students and faculty/staff. In their oft-cited article on the seven principles of good practice in undergraduate education, Chickering and Gamson (1987) declare as their first principle the practice of "encourag[ing] contacts between students and faculty" (p. 3). Several studies identify features and conditions found on individual campuses that foster such contacts.

For example, a campus that fosters student–faculty contact places high value on feedback. In his 2003 book, *The learning paradigm college*, Tagg analyzes the qualities of an institution that has made the shift from a teaching college to a learning college and identifies a professor's feedback as one of the most important features of the "learning college." Tagg first distinguishes feedback from evaluation and then poses three essential qualities of effective feedback.

Feedback, as he defines it, is "about the learner's perceptions and beliefs about his or her performance while evaluation is about perceptions other than the learner's" (2003, p. 185). He explains that under the previous paradigm, the primary function of good faculty was to evaluate the performance of a student and provide him or her clear and useful information. By this standard, students did interact with the professor but only insofar as the evaluative "feedback" was received and understood by the fairly passive student.

The three fundamental characteristics of good feedback add much more to the faculty's role. Tagg declares that good feedback must be *consistent, continual,* and *interactive. Consistent* feedback relates to very clear objectives. What is communicated to the student aligns with course goals, program goals, and even institutional goals.

In turn, *continual* feedback means faculty do as the faculty in the three examples above did: they broadened the means and kinds of connections with students through which information could be meaningfully conveyed. Continual feedback thus involves making use of other contexts, technologies, resources, and people (including other students) in ways that extend meaningful interactions throughout the day and across the campus.

Finally, *interactive* feedback seems self-explanatory because the word itself suggests that both professor and student are communicating. But what could be overlooked is the matter of scale. The interaction needs to happen at a level that is understandable and makes sense to the student.

Tagg certainly is not alone in analyzing the changing nature of ideal feedback. Bok (2006), for example, recounts how starting in the 1970s the preferred role for faculty members giving feedback on student papers has been "less of a critic and proofreader and more of a coach or facilitator" (p. 94). This requires rapport and trust between the student and faculty member.

For feedback to be helpful, its timeliness is essential. Prompt feedback enables students to apply faculty responses to the learning involved in the assignment. Chickering and Gamson identify this as yet another good practice. National studies such as the NSSE and the Wabash National Study, and course-evaluation systems such as the IDEA system,[1] ask students about the frequency with which they have received prompt oral or written feedback from faculty, and then use students' responses to assess the effectiveness of instruction and extent of faculty support of students.

In addition, Kuh et al.'s (2005) study of institutions that document effective educational practice (DEEP) notes that at DEEP institutions feedback is "timely and frequent" (p. 84). Through its data from dozens of institutions, the Wabash National Study documented that prompt feedback, a part of a measure the study calls "Good Teaching and High Quality Interactions with Faculty," promotes student learning.

The Wabash Study identified good teaching and high-quality interactions as one of its four high-impact practices — or the "broad categories of teaching practices and institutional conditions [that] predict growth on a wide variety of student outcomes" (Wabash National Study of Liberal Arts Education, no date). This demonstrates that giving effective feedback is an integral part of good teaching, the topic of the next chapter.

What, specifically, makes student–faculty interaction — including effective feedback — work? In her dissertation, Alderman (2008) found that in high-quality out-of-classroom interactions, faculty members are approachable and personable, care about their students personally, and serve as role models and mentors. She emphasizes: "The most powerful element of high-quality faculty-student out-of-classroom interaction is that of relationship" (p. iv). The importance of "relationship" finds its corollary value in the broadest national studies by Kuh and the authors of the Wabash Study.

As discussed by Kuh et al., student–faculty interactions occur in several institutional programs and practices. Examples are undergraduate research, first-year seminars, and student mentoring or advising. In turn, Alderman categorizes interaction a bit differently, in six types: course-related activities; traveling for conferences or study abroad; casual interactions around campus; career- and graduate-school-focused interaction; visiting faculty in their offices; and participating together in campus clubs or athletic activities.

While most campuses offer plenty of these kinds of venues and opportunities for interaction, extant research also reveals that the kind of interaction described by Kuh et al., authors of the Wabash Study, and Alderman does not happen as often as one would hope. Eagan and his coauthors (2012) cite earlier studies that portray such reality: "Despite the impact of positive student-faculty interactions on student academic success, most students do not interact with faculty frequently (Cotten & Wilson, 2006; Cox & Orehovec, 2007), and such interactions can be especially problematic for students of color to initiate (Nettles, 1990; Hurtado, Eagan, Tran, Newman, Chang & Velasco, 2011)" (p. 2).

In a National Science Foundation funded study of Boise State's STEM courses, Pakala and Haight (2010) identify five primary factors that complicate or hinder good interaction: (1) not enough time; (2) difficult to interact with so many students; (3) not faculty's role to "be friends" with students; (4) interacting with students is not valued by the review system; and (5) formal mentoring is too demanding.[2]

It is quite possible that the conditions described by Eagan, Figueroa, Hurtado, and Gasiewski, and the barriers cited by Pakala and Haight can be as (or more) instructive as the best educational practices cited by Kuh and the Wabash National Study. This is to say, one needs to study both best practices and institutional values that cause barriers and negative conditions. What do faculty and student interviews tell us about what individual faculty can do, even in the presence of such barriers, to make their relationships with students both of high quality and quantity?

CREATING AND SUSTAINING HIGH-QUALITY RELATIONSHIPS WITH STUDENTS

Faculty Commitment to Interaction Depends on Their Perception of Its Value

For faculty to commit to close interaction with students, they first need to be convinced of its value. For example, a physical education instructor who teaches swimming expressed her commitment by saying that she believes it is her role to "help [students] figure out their fear," while several professors highlighted why interaction is important. One reason is that they know that encouraging students and conveying faculty's belief in their students boost the students' confidence.

Many faculty believe that encouragement can positively influence both academics and the student's career choice. One faculty member suggested: "I spend a lot of time cheerleading people, because students really feel that mistakes make them unable to be scientists." Another uses mandatory in-office meetings because he wants to serve as a sounding board for student-created presentation topics, believing it can improve students' reasoning and presentations.

Besides by addressing fear, boosting confidence, and helping students brainstorm, interaction is important because it creates personal connections that not only students appreciate. One professor said, "Typically students just stop me in the hallway asking can I talk to you. I rarely turn them away. That facilitates interaction with students that is more personal." Another said, "Getting to spend time with them outside of class and getting to know other aspects of their lives makes me more sympathetic towards them. It helps me understand them better and enables me to address difficulties in a different way."

And yet another instructor suggested that close interaction in the classroom and lab helps her understand students' learning styles and personalities better and can therefore improve her teaching effectiveness: "Most of the interaction happens in the labs. That is where I talk to students more. I walk around the lab listening and making observations about who is really engaged, who is really loving it. . . . It enables me to see how those who are quieter during lecture interact with their peers. The lab helps me identify students who may be having a hard time."

Student Response to Faculty Commitment

When faculty are convinced of the merits of interaction, and make themselves available, students are willing participants in it, praising the opportunities to get to know their faculty.

Based on the student interviews, it is clear that students sense when faculty are committed to their learning. Thinking about a science professor, one student said, "If she sees that what she is saying doesn't translate well, she keeps explaining until you get it." Students appreciate that faculty "reached out to me," "was always flexible," "receptive to how you understand assignments," and "cared about my learning."

Caring of students' learning, and getting to know students as persons, was a recurring theme across student comments. Such comments are also consistent with Alderman's analysis that part of good interaction is that faculty care about students personally. Students described their faculty that way: "I feel like they are focused on your learning, but also you as a person," noted one student.

Another student's description of a particular faculty member spoke to the importance of students' need to feel welcomed and comfortable around faculty: "She is so approachable and welcoming. I always felt that was really good for a science class in college. Even if it was not about the class, I knew I could go to her. For example, we talked about what I should do in life. I also got to be her teacher's assistant in lab. . . . She made that relationship so solid. I knew I was not interrupting her life, research, or anything."

Benefits of Interaction

Feeling welcomed, comfortable, and encouraged are just some of the benefits students derive from these encounters. One student acknowledged that meeting with the professor "definitely" made it easier to succeed in the class. Another provided an explanation in that outside interaction made him more comfortable to speak up in class. He said that he "definitely see[s] a correlation" between establishing frequent interaction with faculty early in college and his class experience in junior and senior years. Students felt that having a connection with the professor "makes you freer to ask stupid questions."

The personal connections between faculty and students are rewarding for both. Faculty get to know their students, and students get to know "the other side" of faculty, as one professor put it. To him, it is important that students know him not only as a professor of his discipline but also about his extracurricular interests. "I like to have art shows," he says. "I think it is an important thing for people to see — an idea that an economist also paints. I enjoy showing how I live my life."

And students respond. According to one alumnus, such things make professors seem "more human-like." Whenever she has seen that other side of faculty, she says she can further appreciate what they are teaching resulting in greater mutual respect. A question about an ideal instructor yielded similar thoughts in that interaction cannot be a one-way street. It is not only students who learn from the faculty; faculty can learn from students as well, some faculty echoed. Close and personal interaction can give students affirmation and validation.

Also, learning about faculty's interests, background, and experiences can inspire students professionally. One fourth-year business student recalled with admiration a faculty member teaching her during junior/senior year. She had learned that before he started teaching, this professor worked as a trader, after which he started his own hedge fund. "I thought," the student said, "If he can do that, I can, too!"

Another student spoke with admiration of another professor she too had as a junior/senior. This professor used to be Member of Parliament in an African country and now taught students about economic development in Africa. The student was excited that the professor asked her class to come up with "an idea to try and help with development in some country in Africa." This reinforces Alderman's finding that an important part of student–faculty interaction is faculty serving as role models.

Continual, Prompt, and Interactive Feedback

Beyond access, encouragement, and inspiration, how does another important part of the student–faculty relationship — feedback — play out? Several students noted it is very helpful when faculty teach their own labs, enabling students to get more continual feedback. In such cases, the conflict in successive feedback is minimized, as an additional evaluator will not be there to provide different(ly based) evaluation.

Boyer (1987) suggests that it is common that students resent being evaluated by teaching assistants (TAs): "At a large university with many teaching assistants who handle labs and discussion sections, students resent the lack of attention from the professors, suspecting (correctly) that only the T.A. will see and grade their work during the course of the quarter" (p. 142).

Student interviewees also suggested that frequent feedback is helpful. For example, in a history class two different students said the professor always read drafts and gave them very detailed feedback. One of the students said enthusiastically, "That professor is probably single-handedly responsible for taking my writing from high-school level to the college level."

Some faculty members' comments also underline the importance of giving prompt feedback in an interactive way. A physical education professor (quoted above) said:

In PE you have got to give immediate feedback, because, without immediate skill feedback, you will lose the moment. We have struggled
with how best to video tape students as they process and practice their
swimming skills. At the end of a lap I can show the students their
breaststroke. I do not tell them how they performed the skill; I *show*
them their performance. Then I ask them to think, for themselves,
"Does anything need changing? If so, how can you affect that change?"

This professor thinks it is important for students to *participate in identifying their own weaknesses and mistakes,* and in affecting the process of
correcting themselves. Students agree that feedback needs to be given in
an interactive way, as they dislike it when "you get your exam or paper
back, but you don't talk about what you did with the professor."

Individualized Interaction

Implicit in the caring for students personally and providing effective
feedback is the idea that student–faculty interaction should be customized or individualized. Several faculty spoke to this. Comments such as
these were common: "I think about each individual to the extent possible.
I try to have an ability to focus on each individual, to have some idea of
their strengths and weaknesses." This emphasis on individual students
extends from librarians to professors who customize assignments based
on student skills.

For example, a chemistry professor's philosophy is that "if you are a
top-notch student, I give you the highest challenge." (And if a student is
not, the assignment involves more guidance.) This mindset also guides
the questions faculty ask in a classroom setting, as suggested by a biology
professor: "I have to always think about where the students are. I ask
myself, 'What is the next little push I can give them, in the form of
questions as opposed to saying, 'Do this'?'"

And in physical education in which, perhaps more than in other
fields, students feel their limitations and mistakes are "on display for
everyone to see," students can justifiably feel very self-conscious. This is
why the PE professor's strategy must be very individualized: "I do whatever a particular student needs me to do. I have to 'see' what cues can be
most helpful—on the fly—based on what the student's body is doing. I
spend a lot of time watching students under water—that way I can see
what their bodies are doing."

A belief that individualization helps students learn is warranted in the
literature in that the studies that Pascarella and Terenzini (1991) reviewed confirmed that individualization that accommodates different
skill levels and learning styles "consistently appear[s] to produce greater
subject matter learning than do more conventional approaches, such as
lecturing" (p. 646).

Not everyone, however, agrees that individualization is (always) good. Also, many faculty stressed that individual attention does not mean they favor "hand-holding." With reference to students who may be prone to coming up with excuses for late or substandard performance, one professor said: "I tell students that I understand what they are going through but that they have to understand that everybody has problems." The professor added, "You have to help them see that they have to deal with that."

A psychology professor agreed that excessive customization is not good: "I think we are used to this idea of going from mass production to mass customization. Students are thinking that everything should be customized. But I think it is really about translating it for them. Information is not always going to come to you customized; you have to learn how to translate it so that you understand it."

It is important to keep in mind that individual attention is easier to give in certain circumstances that are not present on every campus. For example, it is easier to provide close attention to students on a small campus and in small classes. On a small campus, one student stated, "the campus itself is a classroom. You can see your professors on the quad, at the campus cafeteria, on the tennis court." And when, in addition, the student body consists of lower classmen only, "closer personal relationships with professors happen earlier," as one student put it.

To summarize, for students to be receptive to a rigorous curriculum and demanding courses, while enjoying the learning experience, faculty and students must have a good working relationship, mutual respect, and understanding of each other. That is to suggest that students may learn more when they are challenged and at the same time able to relax in the presence of their professors.

Increasing the number of contexts in which such conversations can occur means the lines distinguishing the academic from the nonacademic and the professional from the personal are blurred so as to enable faculty and students to interact more fully as individuals. This may require thought about where to draw the line between faculty accessibility and student independence on the one hand, and friendship between the two groups and faculty authority on the other. Yet evidence suggests that when an institution is committed to creating and cultivating interactions between students, faculty, and staff, students later recall that such interactions had a positive influence on them, both psychologically/emotionally and in academics.

Indeed, comments by juniors and seniors revealed that close and frequent interaction with their faculty and staff during the freshman and sophomore year was important in setting a fruitful course for, and an anticipation of active involvement with one's teachers during, the rest of their collegiate careers. It was clear that close interactions did not diminish expectations and rigor; rather, they made success more attainable.

NOTES

1. Individual Development and Educational Assessment. This course evaluation system centers on students' self-reports of their learning of specific objectives chosen by the instructor. See http://www.ideaedu.org/services/student-ratings
2. Slide 3 of the authors' PowerPoint presentation.

THREE

Effective Teaching Strategies

While both challenging students and providing them with meaningful, personal interaction with faculty are certainly essential components of effective teaching, there are other, specific strategies that faculty (and staff) can employ to make instruction more effective. We discuss them here, along with the shift in teaching from the delivery of information to the learning paradigm, which has had dramatic impact on teaching itself.

In a 2013 workshop at Oxford College led by Harvard's Eric Mazur, participants got a taste of this shift in one instructor's career. Mazur had always taught physics with joy and exhibited passion to the many topics in his introductory classes. Yet there was a problem. "I was receiving very high evaluations from my Harvard students, but I learned they were actually learning very little of what I was saying." That led him to seek ways to make his teaching more effective.

As the focus in teaching has moved from presentation and delivery to acquisition and learning, a natural consequence has been the development of new pedagogies. In fact, the interviews and focus groups that compose this study reveal at least two significant developments: (1) that of active learning strategies, and inquiry-guided learning in particular; and (2) attention to ways to develop disciplinary thinking. These characterize trends in higher education and the scholarship of teaching and learning.

These two pedagogical efforts are not entirely separate; they share a significant amount of overlap and afford the professor a number of choices for creating the appropriate pedagogy from course to course, discipline to discipline, and even unit to unit.

In this chapter, both the approach used—such as active versus passive learning on the one hand, and attention to discipline-specific learning on the other—and distinct teaching strategies and tactics constitute the high-

impact practice that we call "effective teaching strategies." This HIP sub-
sumes two (sets of) variables used by others: first, excluding the question
on feedback, the Good Teaching composite measure of the Wabash National Study that includes teaching clarity and organization, and second,
two separate principles for good practice in undergraduate education by
Chickering and Gamson (1987): the emphasis on active learning, and the
need to take into account diverse ways of learning. They all relate to good
or effective teaching.

Differently put, while this entire book is about effective teaching, the
current chapter focuses on the above kinds of pedagogies, approaches,
and tactics that teachers can implement (apart from the topics addressed
in other chapters) and that pertain directly to the act of teaching, in and
out of the classroom.

STUDIES AND TRENDS: EFFECTIVE TEACHING

Effective teachers utilize active, or participatory, learning rather than passive learning. Active learning can occur in every discipline, with strategies varying according to course, class size, assignment, and other factors. The central quality is having students perform some task and then
reflect on it (Bonwell & Eison, 1991; Chickering & Gamson, 1987). When
students reflect while reading, writing, discussing, or generally problem
solving (Millis, 2012, p. 1), their minds are more engaged than if they
were just recipients of information.

As Millis reminds us, the insight of early learning theorists like John
Dewey that learning occurs best when students are actively engaged is
confirmed by a number of recent studies of learning and the brain. Active
learning is effective because it gives students the opportunity to question
their assumptions and process their thoughts and doubts more effectively (Boyer, 1987). According to Boyer, "These are the conditions out of
which genuine learning will occur" (p. 159).

The shift to active learning involves a set of strategies named various-
ly as Inquiry, Inquiry-Guided Learning (IGL), Inquiry-Based Learning,
or, as at Oxford College, Ways of Inquiry. It links innate curiosity to
research practices and "inquiry" in the classroom. One generally accepted definition of IGL is that offered by higher-education consultant
Virginia S. Lee: "students' increasingly independent investigation of
questions, problems, and issues, for which there often is no single answer" (2012, p. 6; 2004).

IGL received a strong impetus from the Boyer Commission report of
1998 (The Boyer Commission, 1998), which recommended that research
and inquiry be a much more important part of undergraduate education
at research universities. Since then, IGL has become one of the primary
forms of active learning and has been developed by a number of institu-

tions often in very different ways. For example, McMaster University, North Carolina State, Texas A & M, Penn State, and Oxford College of Emory University (to mention a few) have all developed IGL courses and curricula, each with distinctive features (see Knapper, 2007; Lee, 2004; and Oxford College of Emory University, no date).

McMaster University has offered inquiry-based courses in undergraduate education for twenty years. In New Zealand, where the government mandates the alignment of pedagogy and undergraduate research, a number of institutions have collaborated for more than a decade to develop inquiry guided learning components. In England and the United States, many research institutions have incorporated such components as a way of aligning the curriculum with the fundamental ways knowledge is pursued and constructed by practitioners. In addition to examples of programmatic development of IGL, individual faculty members have developed IGL within their courses.

While the goal of active learning strategies is to strengthen students' ability for independent inquiry, the way in which IGL is often implemented is by using the concepts and tools of specific disciplines. These have to do with, for example, the case method in law school, and, in medicine, learning facilitated by "a senior physician or a resident [who] leads a group of novices through the daily clinical rounds engaging them in discussions about the diagnosis and management of patients' diseases" (Shulman, 2005, p. 52).

In this method, students acquire some of the vocabulary, concepts, and practices of their discipline. Then, "[a]s students gradually and metacognitively recognize the different yet overlapping ways of thinking, knowing, and doing within their different courses, they begin to see a conversation among their courses, allowing them to situate themselves within that conversation and shift from one perspective to another" (Gurung et al., 2008, p. 12). Such "integration of ideas and themes across courses and disciplines enhances critical thinking," as Pascarella and Terenzini put it (1991, p. 158).

In addition to these approaches to learning adopted by an institution and its faculty, faculty can engage in various practices and ways of teaching that maximize learning and student receptiveness. For example, they can respect diverse talents and ways of learning (Chickering & Gamson, 1987), capitalize on learning when students make mistakes (Agrell, 2007), address students' misconceptions (Tanner & Allen, 2005), and make sure they compellingly convey the importance of the material to their students (Boyer, 1987).

EFFECTIVE TEACHING IN PRACTICE

How do effective teachers teach? As Bok (2006) notes, students' learning in college is determined "less by *which* courses they take than by *how* they are taught and *how well* they are taught" (p. 49). The rest of this chapter describes what makes for good teaching, as revealed by faculty and student interviews.

Expectation of Student Participation

One of the primary themes discussed by both faculty and students was the expectation of frequent student participation. Both groups spoke extensively about the positive impact that expectation of student participation had had on student learning. In fact, this was the most frequently brought up theme when students were asked to describe features of teaching that were prevalent in their freshman and sophomore years.

How is an expectation of student participation manifested in practice? One way is the presence of more frequent student presentations and classroom discussion and requiring students to take turns in leading discussion, starting early in the freshman year. A religion professor's strategy, for example, is that "at the beginning of each class, I have a student summarize *and analyze* the previous class meeting. The student needs to tell others the two main points of that class meeting and address implications and limitations. So it is not enough to summarize."

In turn, to ensure that all students participate in class discussion, a philosophy professor urges faculty to pay attention to students' facial expressions and body language. "If you see students changing positions," he says, "you know you will have to change something." Another professor similarly emphasizes reading the students: "If I sense that something is not going right, I tell them, 'Stop, now write x'—and then we will resume discussion."

Through the expectation of student engagement, the interviewed faculty want to develop students' independent thinking and understanding, thus helping them meet the expectation for independent work discussed in chapter 1. In a chemistry professor's words: "I want students to understand what they are doing and *not follow cooking instructions.*" She continues, "If you are following instructions, you are learning how to read an instruction manual, not how to do science. If you give students a worksheet telling them, 'first weigh the metal, then divide the weight by x, and so on,' that is insulting. It is insulting to a third grader!"

She summarizes her philosophy, "What matters is the independence with which students are being asked to solve the problem." To this professor, it is important that she does not share with her students specifics of how to complete the experiments. Instead, she focuses on teaching the principles, goals of the experiments, and how students can think for themselves.

Faculty's belief that participation enhances understanding is also demonstrated by the way the religion professor cited above involves students in the development of his rubrics. He shares with students the rubric categories that should be a part of, for example, a presentation or writing assignment: argument, analysis, sources and documentation, and delivery. He then asks students to explicate on those and define various skills levels. By so doing he tries to "bring special attention to cognitive development." He has found that students' involvement in the development of the rubric enhances their understanding about the types of skills that are necessary to do well in the assignment and how those skills can be demonstrated in practice.

Several students emphasized the positive impact that expectation of participation has had on their confidence. In one student's words, "One of the two things that really stand out [as a take-away from the freshman and sophomore years] is the fact that there was so much emphasis on class discussion. It makes you much more confident when you go out into the real world. Once you're used to sharing your ideas, and with this happening in every class, you no longer stress about it" (white female senior in biology).

Another concurred: "I think class participation was my biggest thing in my early years in college. I broke out of my shell and talked more. Now I don't feel shy being in front of the class and speaking" (a black female junior in business, international student).

Some students spoke of the expectation of engagement in general; others talked about specific teachers who drew them out. They also shared how the expectation of participation helped them learn: "in my biology classes," said one student, "it was very much a dialogue, not just PowerPoint. You learned much more that way."

Emphasis on Student Discovery

One word that several faculty used to describe their purpose for expecting high levels of student participation is student *discovery*. While it is clearly a part of the above chemistry professor's strategy, it applies equally to other disciplines from math and physical education. Faculty spent a lot of time talking about the principle of discovery, aligning with Adler's[1] conclusion that "genuine learning" involves the process of discovery in which the student, not the teacher, is the main agent (cited by Boyer, 1987, p. 150).

In a math professor's career, this has meant that his teaching has evolved from being one-directional, in which he *showed* his students the unexpected connections that math provided, to something much more student-initiated. Previously, he used to ask students, "Do you see how . . . ?" Having adopted the inquiry-guided approach, he now asks, "What do *you* see?" He wants students to discover the unexpected connections that math provides. Teaching this way, he says, it is imperative to "arm students with good questions to ask when approaching the problem. Otherwise students will fall back to what they did in high school— which is memorizing a formula. That is *not* mathematics."

In a swimming class, as suggested by the previous chapter's description of interactive feedback, a professor wants students to analyze their body's movements themselves. She explains: "If a student asks, 'Professor, why am I getting choked?' most teachers would say, 'It is because . . . [proceeding to give them the explanation].' I do not do that. I ask them, 'Why do *you* think you are choking?' I believe students learn better if they discover it for themselves," she stresses. "If they have discovered it, they have learned it."

From Critical Thinking to Intentional Integration

This kind of student independent analysis of processes and problems, whether in math or physical education, often leading to student discovery, is an example of higher-order learning. Higher-order learning involves critical thinking, integration, holistic thinking,[2] and, as a political science professor put it, "diagonal thinking."[3] Faculty spoke quite a bit about critical thinking and integration, which often occur simultaneously. Critical thinking has to do with the evaluation of evidence, while integration can be accomplished by linking one source of data to another, course material to a project or paper, one course to another, and so on.

To practice critical thinking, a biology professor wants students to think about what type of an experiment is needed to produce certain kind of knowledge, and how we know what we know. "I want students not to take knowledge or information for granted," she stresses. Learning to question knowledge is one of the main benefits a senior biology student said she took away from her general education classes: "Now I always question why something works a certain way."

After knowledge and evidence have been evaluated, connecting information from various sources is often the next step. Several faculty, from the physical to social sciences, emphasized the importance of students integrating information they learn in various classes. For example, in a chemistry class "students make compounds that possibly, hopefully, could act as antitumor agents," as its professor explained. "Then," she continued, "in [another chemistry professor]'s class, students test those compounds. They get multiple perspectives on the same research project."

In a physics class, a professor uses the same logic to connect two sequenced courses because she wants students to learn the connections between "what we did last semester and what we are doing now." Her way of accomplishing that is peer instruction. "When students have to teach new things to each other," she says, "they recognize how what they are learning now relates to what they learned in the previous semester." And it is not only faculty who appreciate the linkages between different classes; one student emphasized that "the school connected everything really well. For example, biology connected to other classes. I think liberal arts is like that. It shows how everything is connected."

Distinguishing between Disciplines

While integrating information is one of the earlier steps in the learning process, making conscious and accurate *distinctions* between disciplines can be considered a more advanced one. IGL often entails disciplinary ways of thinking and learning. Such courses are intended to teach students both differences and similarities in how various disciplines produce and process knowledge.

As a good example of differences, a professor of ancient languages explains how ancient languages differ from modern ones, and what the implications are for the classroom:

> In ancient languages you *think* through the language, whereas in other languages, you *feel* through them. Learning ancient languages is such a rational process. That is why there is a lot of burnout. . . . Subconscious/ semiconscious learning that happens in modern language classes (i.e., having fun and learning at the same time) is not going to happen in a Latin class. In an ancient language class it is harder to engage in activities that kind of spontaneously promote learning.

Building Knowledge Systematically

In an ancient language class, as in sciences like biology and chemistry, it is important to build knowledge systematically and gradually. Faculty who teach subjects such as these highlighted that such a systematic method to learning ensures better understanding, retention, and application of knowledge. A biology professor shares the department's philosophy, "We are very thoughtful about starting small and building on that," and similarly a chemistry professor explains that it is important to help students understand the central concepts and principles of the discipline, upon which much of the rest is built.

For example, the central concepts of organic chemistry are structure, polarity, and intermolecular forces. The work of the semester, the professor explains, is "putting the pieces together, building upon the central concepts, branching out from those, going deep, and always coming back to those concepts." A faculty member desiring to use such a strategy would thus first need to identify the central concepts or principles of his or her discipline or course and then develop the syllabus, assignments, and lesson plans around them.

In chemistry, the professor testifies that using the systematic method has resulted in an improved understanding of the discipline by students. Students get frequent exposure to the same concepts and understand how they are linked. The professor shares that based on feedback from instructors in upper-level classes, most students whom she and her colleagues in the department have taught as freshmen and sophomores who go on to major in chemistry exhibit genuine understanding and ability to apply the discipline's concepts in their upper-level courses.

Of course, teaching inquiry, disciplinary thinking, science concepts, or just incorporating more student participation in class in general does not always go smoothly. Faculty need to be prepared for challenges arising both from students and the specifics in the material they teach. For example, a psychology professor's challenge in teaching inquiry guided courses has been that "students are still coming from the approach that teachers are the imparters of knowledge." They expect faculty to give them the answers. Therefore the professor has tried to explain to her students that "we are partners in learning. I feel that if I hold the lectern for sixteen weeks," she adds, "then I have lost the tool for engagement."

Passion and Relevance

There are certain other requirements for students to effectively learn the course material and stay engaged in the classroom. Students need to be motivated to learn the subject matter and engage. This often begins with a knowledgeable and passionate instructor. According to a sociology professor, faculty need to be "exquisitely acquainted with his or her field," have "contagious enthusiasm and passion for the subject," as a math professor put it, and "animate the subject matter in an attractive way, so that students take on the joy that you manifest," as a philosophy professor sees it. The philosophy professor urges his colleagues to use themselves as a conduit for the subject matter. Such an attitude can boost student enthusiasm, while its absence can make it harder to motivate students.

An English professor's experience is that students "know when you are slacking off or when you are not interested in them or in what you are doing." Therefore, he finds it imperative that he does not let himself become disinterested. This becomes increasingly important the longer an instructor has taught a class since "familiarity breeds contempt." Such views by faculty were confirmed by students, who praised instructors who "thoroughly cared about what they were teaching," had "total enthusiasm for the material," and "really knew their stuff."

The interviews revealed that, besides by their attitude, faculty can generate and promote student interest in the subject matter by clearly communicating the relevance of the subject matter. This is particularly important in certain disciplines and courses, in which the usefulness of the material may not be immediately apparent. This is what a math instructor brought up early in his interview: "Especially in math, you have to win students' hearts before you can teach their minds. . . . They see math as very gray, with a lot of numbers, and not interesting. What I am trying to help them see is that math is not just a bunch of numbers but something that can reveal something interesting when scratched and looked into deeper."

Another math professor shared a similar priority in establishing subject matter relevance, as revealed by the aims of his two-page essay assignment: "Interdisciplinary connections is certainly one of them. . . . Math is applicable to so many things. I try to get students outside of the microcosm, or whatever nutshell they are in, and show how math is connected to nature, or whatever the case may be. So part of my purpose is to help the students see the world in terms of the math they are studying."

One of the student interviewees explained why subject matter relevance is so important: "I feel like you can learn as much as you want, but if you can't associate what you learn with real life, to life outside of school, it doesn't help you much. I relate the things I learn in one class to another. That's what I'm gonna take away from my classes."[4]

Creative and Fun Assignments

One of the primary ways students learn course content is through assignments. Students are more likely to stay engaged with assignments that are creative and fun. Both faculty and students shared several examples of these. In one, a sociology class called Social Problems, students learn about social problems first hand by spending a week observing and participating in real-life problem solving in various locations and facilities in inner-city Atlanta. This includes riding with police officers on night patrol in a poor neighborhood, visiting an intensive-care unit of a public hospital, and feeding the elderly in an Alzheimer's unit.

In the last setting, the professor describes that, sometimes while they are being fed, some of the elderly patients forget that they are eating. "There are tears and anxiety," he describes students' reaction. His goal for the course is that students "experience things that are not immediate but that are part of the landscape they have to deal with. It produces people who are thoughtful."

He also teaches a medical sociology class, in which he has a similarly creative, action-oriented assignment with real-life application. He asks students to break into three-person groups and go to Kroger, a local grocery store. Before they go, he gives them a list of five prepared foods, such as Smucker's jam, for which he then asks students to record the ingredients and "the published, empirical health implications of those ingredients." He then asks students to teach those implications to the class. "They are appalled," he describes students' reaction, continuing, "What has to happen, maybe in a visceral way, is that students have to stop sleep walking and realize that the vast majority of items in the grocery store is rubbish."

Yet another example of a creative assignment with which students often connect comes from Abnormal Psychology. Students are asked to choose an autobiography of a person who has had a significant amount of problems or stress in his or her life. They have to pretend that the person is their client and then write an Intake Report to diagnose him or her. Students find the assignment fascinating, learning how complex psychological abnormalities can be.

The professor says students learn empathy: "When they merely read diagnoses, it is hard for them to get a sense of what it is like to live with that disorder. But when they read the autobiographies, having to pretend the person is their client, they begin to understand that." He has thus found that creative and participatory assignments drive home his lessons more effectively than ones in which students carry only a passive role.

Emotional Identification with the Subject Matter

The effectiveness of assignments like these, an interviewed language professor would say, comes from students' "emotional identification with the subject matter." In such assignments, faculty are aware of and nurture the emotional component of learning. "Every form of innovative pedagogy that I have used has an emotional component," the professor emphasizes. He explains that such a component is especially important in courses that are inherently repetitive (for example, introduction to a language). It helps students stay excited. And most importantly, every time students have identified with the subject matter emotionally, the professor has found that quality of student work has improved noticeably.

Most recently this happened in a class in which students had to relate the message of Virgil's *Aeneid* to the lives of local war veterans whom students were assigned to interview. "The most important outcome was that the students' papers were all good," the professor recalls. "Even the mechanics of writing were better." By interviewing veterans, students identified with the course text and became much more involved in the assignment. "When students have so much to say in their papers," the professor learned, "the mechanical errors go away. When they really care about the topic, the outcome is better in every way. It all goes back to the emotional attachment to the subject matter."

Yet, while these assignments from sociology, psychology, and Latin show how faculty can make learning fun and exciting, another professor

expressed the other side of the coin when it comes to creative assignments. She declared,

> I think there is a little bit too much emphasis on how the teacher can
> make the material engaging. The students, too, need to find a way for
> education to be interesting for them. Otherwise life will be miserable
> for them. They have their responsibility too! If you just think about
> education as a way to get a high-paying job, your four years of educa-
> tion will be misery. They should think, "Let me find out why this
> teacher finds thermodynamics, for example, interesting!"

Helping Students Know What They Know

Engaged learning, especially if it succeeds in producing critical thinking and other higher-order skills, combined with instructor knowledge
and passion for the subject matter, form the foundation for effective
teaching. What else should faculty do to steer students toward deep
learning? One theme that arose in the interviews is the importance of
faculty helping students become aware of what they know, what they do
not know, and where they may be misinformed.

That is why a political science professor pointed out that administer-
ing a final exam at the end of the semester and just asking students pick
up their graded exams without a conversation with the instructor is not
an effective practice. There is no guarantee that students will read the
instructor's feedback. He explained, "Finding out what students know is
not good teaching. Helping *them* find out what they know is good teaching." This relates to the important theme of feedback, as discussed in
chapter 2. While feedback is a form of support for the student, it is certainly also an integral part of effective teaching.

Addressing Students' Misconceptions

A physics professor argued that another, related, effective practice is:

> getting students to discuss their misconceptions. Students often think
> that in science there is no discussion, that there is a correct answer, that
> things are black and white. Often, there *is* a correct answer, of course.
> However, it is important to understand the process of science, not just
> the answers. I want my students to see how certain concepts have
> needed to be introduced, both in our classes and historically. I want
> them to understand why, historically, physicists have concluded that
> the concepts that were already well understood were not enough to
> describe certain phenomena and that therefore, new concepts were
> needed for the explanation.

Such a goal applies to teaching other disciplines, too. In religion, a
professor calls discussing student misconceptions "bias clarification" and
finds it necessary in his discipline: "by and large, students have not stud-

ied religion academically." He thinks it is important for students to get a revelation of their misconceptions and prejudices.

In psychology, there is similarly often a need to clarify certain beliefs, which a professor does through his "myth busters assignment." Below the professor describes his assignment, demonstrating how students in Introductory Psychology proceed through it:

> Students form teams of two, and draw a myth from a big bag of myths about psychology that I have prepared in advance. Some are true, some false; some are partly true and partly false. An example: "We only use ten percent of our brain." I have about fifty of these examples. The idea is that students are not only supposed to find out whether the myth is true but also to learn about ways to investigate the answer.

The professor continues:

> There are five or six different things I ask them to do while investigating their myth: (1) describe what they initially thought about the myth; (2) conduct a poll of their friends and analyze the poll; (3) go to "Ask Yahoo" and poll the Internet to see what others think about the myth; (4) analyze discussion boards/blogs about the topic; (5) review newspaper articles or books; and (6) review one research article about it. They have to do all of these. Early on, we bring in someone from the library to teach them how to use the databases.

At the end of the semester, the professor explains, students present their findings to the class. In these presentations, they have to share what they discovered through each of the six ways of knowing. With the bulk of evidence, students then have to decide whether the myth is true or not.

The benefit of the assignment, the professor shares, is that "all throughout the semester, when we talk about research methods, students have *their* data that they have collected and that they can talk about. So they are not talking about random correlations, but correlations they have seen in their data." Besides helping students investigate myths and clarify their biases, this example of engaged learning teaches students to work together, critically evaluate and integrate evidence, question their assumptions, reflect on what they have observed, and hone in on their presentation skills.

Removing Students from Their Usual Contexts

Another way for faculty to "bust myths" is by removing students from their usual contexts, as one professor put it. According to this English professor, changing contexts in which learning occurs and letting students observe people and conditions that are different from their own backgrounds and experiences can help broaden students' perspectives and values—addressing prejudices as well. In her interdisciplinary honors seminar, Rhetoric on Incarceration in the United States, this professor takes students to a women's maximum security prison and asks them to evaluate the justification for, or correctness of, students' thoughts about incarceration. "What I think that they are learning is that our values are contextual," she has observed.

Creating Surprise in the Classroom

Faculty may also incorporate a surprise element inside the classroom via activities that "keep students on their toes," as another English professor does. The benefit, as in the prison visits, is a certain shock effect that can help keep students interested (and awake). This professor does not want his students to always think they know what is going to happen in class on a given day. "Invariably," he says, "there will be a certain rhythm to the course, a certain pace—for example, an essay every other week. Yet I want students to be aware that something entirely different could happen. This is to prevent them from becoming too habituated to the course, enabling them to tune out," he says. "It is to counteract boredom. I try to surprise them whenever I can."

Surprising students can be accomplished, among other things, by asking unexpected questions, or leading students to unexpected connections, as in the math example mentioned earlier, or "asking questions sideways," as yet another English professor put it. Her experience is that a lot of her students come to class "ready to turn in a five-paragraph paper." She wants to ask her students questions they are not used to. Especially with common texts like *Pride and prejudice*, she explains, this means asking questions that are unusual—"so that they really need to think about them for themselves."

Strategic Use of Mistakes

As advocated by Agrell (2007), the interviewed faculty also strategically incorporate student mistakes into the learning process, guiding students so that they maximize learning from their mistakes and failures, whether the failures result from prejudice, ignorance, or lack of effort, or are just part of the normal learning process.

A science professor explains how she does this. Learning from one's mistakes is how science works anyway, she stresses:

> Many times students' misconceptions will lead students to the wrong choice. I firmly believe that you need to let students go there. When their misconceptions lead to something wrong, their brain goes, "Wait a minute," and they really have to think about it. You need to reduce the complexity of the task, but you still need to make the pieces challenging. What you do in graduate school is all about why things do not work. Then when something does work, you *know* why.

In turn, an English professor wants her students to understand that "if you start over, it is not a bad thing. It says, 'My standards are higher than this.' Otherwise," she says, "they write a two-to-three-page paper that is unfixable" and uninteresting. Thus, while it is normal that students learn from their mistakes, this pedagogy is a conscious awareness raising about the benefit of making mistakes, as well as leading students to set high standards for themselves.

Faculty can also utilize mistakes in another way. For example, an economics professor challenges students by using "catch me in the error" assignments, in which students get extra points for identifying an intentional error that the professor has injected into her lecture. The professor finds that students are really excited when they identify the error and notes that this tactic is one among many that she uses to communicate high expectations.

Considering Diverse Ways of Learning

The final theme that arose in faculty and student conversations on effective teaching practices is the need for faculty to take into account diverse ways of learning (Chickering & Gamson, 1987). Faculty does this by using different kinds of assignments, assessments, and interaction to address differences in student skills, backgrounds, and ways of learning. For example, every exam that a political science professor administers in his Introduction to Politics class includes a range of question types—identifications or a short essay question, a comprehensive component, and some short-answer questions.

A math professor uses a similar strategy: "You try to have different kinds of assessments and even on the same test different kinds of questions, timed and nontimed. You build some kind of variety into testing. I am conscious of selecting different kinds of problems—short answer, multiple choice, writing/explaining, and quizzes that students take home."

Students appreciate this. One praised a biology professor who used different kinds of assignments, who "tried to do visual, hands-on, and other types of assignments, for every type of learner."

Another way to address diverse learning styles is simply to try and work with students individually, as much as possible, yet keeping in mind the downside of excessive customization, as stressed in chapter 2. The above math professor explains his strategy: "It is important for me to listen well. All my life I have practiced and tried to improve listening. I do not just listen to people's words; I try to understand how they are feeling and what is motivating them to say what they are saying."

Common to these many examples of effective teaching strategies is that they make learning personal. All of the following speak to the fact that students learn best when they connect with the course material personally: subject matter relevance, emotional identification with the subject matter, the importance of helping students know what they know and what they do not know, and the intentional use of student mistakes and failure to help students learn. Another theme—clear in the emphases on engaged learning, classroom participation, and independent inquiry—is that students learn best by doing.

So, on the one hand, faculty have the responsibility to help students see the connection of the course material to students' lives and break the learning process into steps—such as by introducing the central concepts or principles of their discipline, and showing how these concepts are linked. But on the other, students need to be given responsibility for their learning. Through inquiry, students can engage in the process of discovery and meaning making.

And yet a third element of what makes teaching effective is what students perceive simply as the "personality" of the instructor. Some faculty talked about their teaching being most effective when they taught the way that suits them and that is comfortable for them—as opposed to emulating others.

So good teaching appears to be a combination of the ability to implement best practices, while staying true to one's style and personality as a teacher. One of these best practices is inquiry-guided learning. With data suggesting that this method produces greater levels of learning, it is probably a good idea for faculty to seek to increase student independence (when circumstances allow for that), utilize activity and reflection, and direct students to ask their own questions of the material to which they are exposed. The natural extension and a particular example of this is to engage students in undergraduate research, which will be the topic of the next chapter.

NOTES

1. Adler, M. J. (1982). *The Paideia Proposal: An educational manifesto*. New York, NY: Macmillan, p. 23.

2. A political science professor defined this as the practice of referencing several disciplines to understand and develop one's worldview.

3. In diagonal thinking, students connect "how one part of the class fits other parts or other classes."

4. The importance of the relevance of course material to students' lives will be further discussed in chapter 6.

FOUR

The Undergraduate Research Experience

Undergraduate research brings together the themes of the previous three chapters in that good and challenging teaching involves research experiences for students; undergraduate research is also an extension of active and engaged learning strategies. Furthermore, it brings students into close contact with their professors.

Undergraduate research—or "individual projects supervised by faculty members and collaborations with faculty mentors," can be considered part of an effective teaching strategy, since the literature confirms that through such projects students acquire research skills and problem-solving skills and a "greater satisfaction with the educational experience" (Brownell & Swaner, 2009b, pp. 4–5). But since it is one of the AAC&U's high-impact practices, it is discussed separately in this chapter.

Undergraduate research also connects to learning in the disciplines. In the distant past, the work of the disciplines was separate from classroom work and course syllabi, especially for undergraduates. Undergraduate students filled large lecture halls, absorbed as much raw information as possible, and gave the information back to professors on fact-based exams.

In some disciplines, the traditional library-research-paper process could incorporate aspects of disciplinary research. Yet courses and programs that entail disciplinary research and that can be called undergraduate research are normally different from traditional library research. In addition to the invaluable skills usually acquired by students in library research such as database search, evaluation of sources, citation, and most importantly critical thinking, undergraduate research carries with it the added feature of original and often student-generated research projects.

This chapter briefly outlines trends and lessons learned in analyses on undergraduate research, followed by examples of best practices in faculty implementation of undergraduate research.

TRENDS, PRACTICES, AND PAST STUDIES IN UNDERGRADUATE RESEARCH

Undergraduate research programs trace back to a time when faculty selected a few fortunate gifted students to work with on faculty's current research projects. Research institutions like Massachusetts Institute of Technology (MIT) developed a more systematic and comprehensive approach. In 1969, the Undergraduate Research Opportunities Program (UROP) at MIT and gradually at other research institutions started offering students the opportunity to participate in faculty research projects.

After The Boyer Commission report *Reinventing undergraduate education* (1998) challenged research institutions to develop further research opportunities for students in order to promote key capacities and skills of critical thinking, many universities developed undergraduate research programs. In a 2012 survey by *US News and World Report* (as part of its rankings assessment), academic leaders at 1,500 institutions were asked to send a list of the top ten undergraduate research/creative work programs.[1]

The twenty-five institutions that received most mention spanned the academic spectrum from private research universities like Cal Tech, Duke, and Stanford to state institutions like University of Arizona and University of North Carolina, to small liberal arts colleges like Carleton, Elon, and the College of Wooster. This range demonstrates the growing success and popularity of undergraduate research programs in nearly every academic context. One scholar describes the phenomenal growth as moving from a "cottage industry to a movement" (Blanton, 2008, p. 233).

It is difficult to identify universal key features of a "typical" undergraduate research program. Many are run in the summer, but there are also very good programs that span the academic year. One fundamental criterion is the mentoring relationship between students and faculty, either one-to-one or with small groups of students working on a project.

Also, while anchored in the expertise or ongoing research of the faculty, projects are often student-initiated. Students can present their findings at a research symposium, and a number of good undergraduate journals offer students the opportunity to submit an article to a peer-reviewed journal. Students who participate in these programs are frequently rising juniors through seniors completing their capstone experience. These programs have traditionally been more common in the natural sciences.

Consequently, one concern during the development of undergraduate research programs has been to expand the programs' reach to other disciplines, including the humanities. In a 2008 article, Schantz delineates the key challenges in developing humanities projects in undergraduate research programs: (1) necessary long apprenticeships, (2) lack of neat contained projects that can be found in the natural sciences, and (3) the noncollaborative nature of many projects in the humanities.

Humanities research is overwhelmingly the enterprise of an individual scholar who studies a particular question within a narrowly defined area in order to produce a clear answer to the question. Schantz goes on to describe the need for more collaborative research projects in the humanities, a need that the Associated Colleges of the South (ACS), a consortium of small liberal arts colleges, is exploring.

Assessing the impact of undergraduate research programs on student learning has been another challenge, particularly in an era of budget cuts and spiraling costs. Surveys, focus groups, and other qualitative data have given administrators and program directors insights into the perceived learning that such programs foster.

Using University of Georgia data, a study by Fechheimer, Webber, and Kleiber (2011) asks, "How well do undergraduate research programs promote engagement and success of students?" and finds that students who are involved in undergraduate research courses and programs for more than a semester see an increase in their GPA. The authors also summarize the findings of others, including Lopatto (2004, 2007, 2009),[2] who found in the context of "more than 100 institutions and 3000 students," that the Summer Undergraduate Research Experience (SURE) "promotes gains in skills, self-confidence, pathways to science careers, and active learning" (Fechheimer et al., 2011, p. 156).

They continue to report, "Gains in skills, scientific understanding, self-confidence, and commitment to science and research have been reported in numerous studies (Holt & Kleiber, 2001; Bauer & Bennett, 2003; Seymour et al., 2004; Russell, 2008; Trosset et al., 2008)" (pp. 156–57). Undergraduate research has also been found to increase students' likelihood of enrolling in graduate school (Brownell & Swaner, 2009a).

One feature that is particularly pertinent in the current study is research programs for first- and second-year students, which a smaller number of institutions have developed. These programs often work to meet other institutional goals, such as student retention. At the University of Kentucky, for example, the first-year research program serves the twin purposes of improving retention and engagement (Marcus et al., 2010).

In turn, the Undergraduate Research Scholars program at the University of Wisconsin at Madison is "dedicated to enhancing the academic experience of UW-Madison students by providing first and second year undergraduates with opportunities to earn credit for participating in the research and creative work with UW-Madison faculty and staff" (University of Wisconsin-Madison, no date). And Miami University offers a learning community, the First Year Research Experience, to give students an opportunity to not only engage in research their first year but also to find a faculty mentor early in the college career (Miami University-Ohio, no date).

INSTITUTIONAL AND FACULTY STRATEGIES IN UNDERGRADUATE RESEARCH INSTRUCTION

Some institutions have answered the challenge by The Boyer Commission to provide research opportunities in the first college year in a very clear way by constructing research experiences for every student. One way to do this is by requiring each student to take a certain number of inquiry courses in various disciplines, as these courses have an emphasis upon individual and small-group inquiry projects that are frequently based in disciplinary research protocols and the ways knowledge is pursued in the discipline.

Authentic Research at the Introductory Level

As with any good educational practice, the effective implementation of it depends first on the value that faculty place on it. Virtually all of the interviewed faculty indicated that they place high value on the development of student research skills and involving all students in research. For this to happen, though, appears to be dependent on the adoption of high expectations in general, and, on the other hand, the practice of inclusion and equal treatment of students—faculty belief that students at all levels should be exposed to and trained in research.

Biology professor #1 explains: "We have for quite a while been trying to engage our students in independent research—authentic research at the introductory level. This investment used to be a prerogative of only a few students. . . . But our approach in biology is that every student should engage and develop in it. It is not to say they are doing ground breaking, independent research, but they are all engaged in it."

The professor elaborates by saying that expecting research from all students is now really one of the big goals in undergraduate science education. She says that her department does it for the nonmajors too, although in a more limited way "that gives them a feel for the scientific process."

As suggested, there is a positive relationship between the setting of high expectations in general and faculty expectations regarding research in particular. The professor continues: "In some settings faculty view introductory biology students as not ready for primetime," but adds that her department does not view students that way. "We have an intentional appreciation for the abilities of first and second-year students."

Shared Excitement about the Subject Matter

Part of this appreciation is that faculty share with students the "excitement of biology," which faculty may in some other contexts think of as their prerogative. In this professor's view, shared excitement is really much more important than support. This refers to shared experience of learning, sharing information, and answering questions. She believes that this leads to students wanting to learn more. When students feel appreciated, she says, they want to understand. "They want to be a part of the process."

Viewing Students as Capable, Valuing Their Input

Sharing excitement about the subject matter with students presupposes that students are mature enough to appreciate such excitement. Biology professor #2 notes that in her experience, most faculty on campus want to view their students as mature and capable, even when there may be initial hurdles in getting students to think and operate at a higher level. "I have to constantly check myself," she says, "against thinking, 'Oh well, students are just not bright enough; they do not know how to work hard enough.'" She says she tries very hard to get away from that.

The viewpoint that this suggests is that this professor desires to see her students as partners in research. Yet she is quick to add:

> I am not thinking that students will be my fellow researchers. I think the better way to describe it would be that they make me think in a different way. It is not that they must have the skills of a researcher and be able to do something completely amazing on their own. I always have to keep in mind that these are freshmen and sophomores. But I have the expectation that they can think, even at that age, at a level at which they would think with more experience. The challenge is how to get them to *start* to think that way.

To this professor, undergraduate research represents an opportunity both to faculty and students: to her, it is an opportunity for greater fulfillment in her career, while to students it is a way to grow in their skills and confidence. She stresses that both groups need to benefit from it. That is why she does not select for her research projects students who have not taken a class with her. "If they have taken a class with me I know they are really interested in science. That helps ensure that it will be an effective partnership."

These comments speak to the importance that faculty place on being intentional about valuing student input. A political science professor calls such an attitude "respecting students' minds." In this line of thought, faculty ought not to treat students as, again, receptors of knowledge and information, but as contributors. While students are not considered equals, their opinions and experiences are valued—which the institution and faculty can demonstrate by, among other things, giving students undergraduate research opportunities.

The political science professor explains how this works: "If I interact with students and show them what they are doing and then listen to their views, whether they are verbal or written, I am respecting their minds. If, on the other hand, all I am doing is reading what they have written and grade it, and the students themselves do not know if it is good enough, it is like gambling for them, a roulette."

What else does an attitude of respecting students' minds look like? The professor gives an answer that connects with the tenets of inquiry-based learning, in which students contribute to the production and evaluation of knowledge. Respecting students' minds happens when "we can have a discussion where we are really talking, without me being the fount of knowledge." Echoing the biology professor's view, he continues, "It is not that I am equal with the students. We are not all the same in the classroom. *But,* you can raise the students to a point where they can actually see that they have something worthwhile to say and that they can interact at a level at which they are not used to interacting."

Such a mindset requires a certain level of humility on the part of the faculty member. "If you do not walk into a classroom honestly believing that you can very well encounter someone who is smarter than you are," the above professor continued, "you cannot be a good teacher. Students will not be more educated than you are, but they could be smarter."

Several other faculty stressed the importance of faculty attitude toward student input. A sociology professor emphasized meeting students where they are, after which, "you set the occasion for them to evolve as a young intellect. You do not condescend them; you do not dismiss them; you do not interrupt them. You take them seriously as a young evolving scholar. You invest in them."

And in an English professor's words: "The students are so young, and some of them so uncertain, that it is very important and impactful that I show them I take their ideas seriously and that their ideas are worthwhile."

Faculty seemed truly intentional about expressing their appreciation of and seriousness with which they approached students' contributions—making this the primary theme in the interviews concerning faculty approach to undergraduate research. This comes back to the type of student–faculty relationship that is "high impact." It also comes back to the idea of undergraduate research as being a partnership between faculty and students, as opposed to a more one-directional mentoring relationship.

To maximize both exposure to and learning from undergraduate research, it seems helpful to have multiple opportunities available for students that are disciplinary, authentic, and original in a variety of contexts ranging from the traditional undergraduate research programs (for example, SURE) to an honors seminar and the presence of required inquiry-guided learning courses. This availability should combine with faculty attitude of seriousness toward student input and availability for and encouragement of students.

This way, faculty serve as partners, role models, and support network for young scholars in their maneuvering through and learning about the research process. This can have not only academic but important psycho-emotional benefits as well, as revealed by one student who said with pride in her voice: "My most meaningful experiences [during the freshman and sophomore years] came when I was engaged. On a two-year campus, when you're a sophomore you're a PI [Principal Investigator]. We sophomores were the ones who had to evaluate and reevaluate if something didn't work."

Her comment also attests to the spirit of community and collaboration among students, another theme that arose when students were asked about what helped them learn, whether in research assignments or in general, during their first years in college. Therefore, collaborative assignments, which are intricately tied to leadership development, will be the topic of the next chapter.

NOTES

1. http://colleges.usnews.rankingsandreviews.com/best-colleges/rankings/undergrad-research-programs. Accessed July 20, 2013.

2. Lopatto, D. (2004). Survey of undergraduate research experience (SURE): First findings. *CBE—Life Sciences Education, 3*, 270–77; Lopatto, D (2007). Undergraduate research experiences support science career decisions and active learning. *CBE—Life Sciences Education, 6*, 297–306; Lopatto, D. (2009). *Science in solution: The impact of undergraduate research on student learning.* Tucson, AZ: The Research Corporation for Science Advancement.

FIVE
Collaborative Learning and Leadership Development

Undergraduate research, discussed in the previous chapter, may not involve collaboration with peers, but it could. In general, there is much overlap between collaborative learning and the other high-impact practices, such as in the emphasis on active learning: collaborative work "places the responsibility for students' learning on the students themselves" (Millis, 2010, p. 6).

Another reason that collaborative assignments—such as in-class group projects and research with others—are "high impact" is that they force students to "sharpen . . . [their] thinking and deepen . . . [their] understanding" (Chickering & Gamson, 1987, p. 3). To complete a collaborative assignment successfully, students must "listen . . . seriously to the insights of others, especially those with different backgrounds and life experiences" (Kuh, 2008, p. 10). Only by seeking to understand each other and working together can students bring a collaborative assignment into a coherent whole.

This chapter discusses collaboration in conjunction with leadership development because leadership is intricately connected to a group's ability to work together, enabling participants to get things done. In fact, in many higher-education institutions leadership is understood in reference to *working with others to reach common goals—toward social change*. In this sense the ability to collaborate and lead can be treated synonymously.

Therefore, "leading" is not to be equated merely with holding a leadership position. It involves serving as a role model for others, but also consulting others for input. Such leadership facilitates fruitful collaboration and achievement of the group's goals. Therefore, this chapter understands leadership in the context of teamwork; leadership can, but does not have to, involve a formal leadership role. Leaders inspire both self and others, with "others" consisting of both a working group/organization to which one belongs and one's community. On campus, students can develop leadership skills in both curricular and extracurricular contexts.[1]

Below, the chapter briefly reviews the development and use of collaboration as pedagogy, the benefits of collaborative learning, and some research on leadership experience. It then shares examples of how faculty can use, and help students benefit from, collaborative learning, as well as develop student leadership skills. It also discusses how students experience and interpret collaboration with their peers and leadership opportunities.

THE DEVELOPMENT AND USE OF COLLABORATION AS PEDAGOGY

During the late 1980s through the 90s when a full exploration of a number of active-learning strategies began, developing small-group assignments and activities came into focus. In addition to learning course content (the terms, concepts, and processes of given courses within each discipline) students began to be asked to *do* something with that information and then to *reflect* on what happened and what they learned.

In elementary and secondary education, the movement took the form of "cooperative learning" in which the teacher retained most of the authority while putting students to work on tasks in small groups while the knowledge and skills of the teacher remained the final stage of the process. In the university setting, a more ambitious undertaking evolved in which students collaborated together more independently of the professor in efforts not only to discern the correct answers or solutions but in teaching each other and developing knowledge on their own.

Some early discussion ensued over collaborative and cooperative learning, the two terms used quite interchangeably today to describe the pedagogy that relies on students working together. According to Panitz (1999), collaborative learning requires students to be more independent and at a more advanced stage of learning.[2]

He distinguishes further key differences. Whereas *cooperative* learning has as its primary goal the achievement of a specific task, *collaborative* learning is more a lifestyle or way to approach all learning and is especially useful in courses that pose more open-ended, "unanswerable" questions. So the distinction is found in the degree of independence expected of students and the kinds of problems with which students are challenged.

Collaborative or cooperative learning often utilizes small groups. In a composition class, these groups may acquire the name of "peer editing group" while in biology, a small peer group may form in the lab setting. Small teams of students may develop case-study presentations in government, history, or political science, engage in "think-pair-share" activities, or debate issues.

Group learning in class may also involve simply working together through a question posed by the instructor, or then combining that with more creativity in role playing or playing games (Paulson & Faust, no date).

In these settings, we find "small groups working on specific tasks" in various ways (Millis, 2002, p. 1). Millis (2010) reports that faculty use the term "cooperative learning" to apply to a wide range of pedagogies and course units—process-oriented guided inquiry in chemistry, interactive lectures in statistics, or sequencing of assignments in literature classes.

One important aspect to consider in using collaborative learning in class is group composition. In Shadle's (2010) course in general chemistry, this refers to the "structure that students need to have confidence in the course" (p. 38). She spends a great deal of time planning the groups of students, creating heterogeneous groups in which students' strengths and weaknesses can challenge those of others and support each other's learning. In this way, students learn to depend on each other for accurate and necessary information in order to progress in the course. This cooperative arrangement augments learning and supports the building of community in the course.

BENEFITS OF COLLABORATIVE LEARNING

Research has shown that small groups of students working together with clear direction and support from the professor frequently learn more deeply and are motivated by interacting with each other to teach others within the group as well. For example, in their extensive report about the history, use, and benefits of cooperative learning, Johnson, Johnson, and Smith (1991) point out, "The more one works in cooperative learning groups, the more that person learns, the better he understands what he is learning, the easier it is to remember what he learns, and the better he feels about himself, the class, and his classmates" (p. 8).

In turn, in *Our underachieving colleges*, Bok (2006) addresses similar benefits citing the same authors, but emphasizes that the mere existence of a group is not enough:

> Simply assigning tasks to groups . . . is not sufficient. For optimum results, participating students need to recognize that each depends on the others for a favorable result; collaboration must be face-to-face; each member of the group must be held accountable in some fashion (to avoid free riders); and members should periodically discuss how

each has contributed to the final product and how each could help to make the group even more effective (p. 118).

Thus for optimum results both for the project and participants, cooperation must be multidirectional, with all members participating. In Johnson et al.'s (1991) words, participation in activities such as think-pair-share, peer reviews, and projects promotes "positive interdependence" (p. 25).

Citing Pascarella and Terenzini (1991), Bok (2006) quantifies the extent to which students learn more when collaborating compared to when working alone: "Where these [the above] conditions exist, the great majority of studies show that participating students make much greater gains (approximating half of a standard deviation) over those achieved by classmates studying individually or competing with one another for grades or other prices" (p. 118).

In particular, Gokhale (1995) has demonstrated that these gains occur mainly in the critical-thinking skills of students working collaboratively in small groups. But students working in groups also gained in practical skills.

Students learn more through collaboration because, first, collaboration involves doing—and people learn more by doing than merely by listening or taking notes. Also, as mentioned, it forces students to listen to others' viewpoints, sharpen their thinking, and deepen their understanding. Paulson and Faust suggest this is also because it "encourage[s] discussion of problem solving techniques ('Should we try this?,' etc.)" (no date, p. 9). The authors also emphasize that through debates, students learn argumentation skills.

Yet benefits of collaboration do not extend to intellectual development, academics, or even concrete skills alone. Other benefits can include enhanced self-esteem (Johnson et al., 1991), and, "[w]here groups are mixed by race," reduced prejudice, and better adjustment to college (Bok, p. 118). This may happen because through an effective use of cooperative strategies, faculty can help "build community and foster engagement" (Millis, 2010, p. 4). Through an increased understanding of others, benefits of collaboration may also extend farther, to one's environment, community, and society.

In fact, Boyer (1987) suggests that for *democracy* to function effectively, students need to collaborate. Putnam would agree: in his famous work on the decline of social capital and collaboration in the United States, he makes the point that the trend he calls "bowling alone" is a result of a decline in community participation (1995; 2000). Similarly, the reason he argues democracy *works* in northern Italy is because of a *high* level of engagement in community associations, through which people have learned to trust each other (Putnam, 1993). Collaboration therefore has potential implications that go far beyond the individual student.

RESEARCH ON LEADERSHIP EXPERIENCE

Regarding the beneficial impact of leadership experience, research has established that formal leadership positions, too, have a role to play in student development. This may be because holding a formal leadership role positions students to practice the kind of leadership in which they serve as examples and learn to cooperate effectively.

In fact, in their review of research on the effects of college, Pascarella and Terenzini (1991) share a fascinating finding by Pascarella, Ethington, and Smart (1988)[3] who compare various experiences in college: "'Social leadership' experiences (such as being president of a student organization, serving on committees, being involved in a play) had *the only consistently positive and significant direct effect* on students' humanitarian and civic values nine years after college" (p. 311).

This is to say that leadership experiences produce caring humans. In fact, Astin et al. (2011) note that leadership *training* too produces it—the "ethic of caring," or in other words, empathy and understanding of others (p. 148). It helps students "develop the skills of collaboration with others in solving and in leading organizational efforts" (ibid, p. 148[4]). And, like collaboration, this is then likely to affect students' societal and community behavior as well.

This is a significant outcome. In his discussion about the aims of education, Bok (2006) stresses that not many would argue today that the only purpose of universities and colleges is to improve students' intellectual capabilities. Rather, universities and colleges should also help develop students' moral character, civic participation, and other such virtues.

TEACHING AND LEARNING COLLABORATION AND LEADERSHIP

The ways in which professors implement collaborative work in the class include small-group strategies listed earlier in this chapter. For example, in biology a professor walks around in class, observing the extent to which groups whose task is to solve a problem relying on information learned in a previous class work together, without one or a few members dominating.

Assigning such group work requires certain logistics and probably more time than traditional assignments. An ongoing challenge is group composition and formation, such as whether groups should be determined by the instructor or freely formed by students. Three of the interviewed faculty mentioned that they prefer heterogeneous groups (and therefore assigning group members), and two emphasized their use of the same groups throughout the semester.

This heterogeneity can address gender, background, and ability, but also worldview, if known to faculty. For example, an economics professor (economics professor #1) deliberately assigns groups in which students hold different views regarding economic policy. "I intentionally form groups that are very diverse," he says, "building into them diverse viewpoints so that in a discussion group there are students of both conservative and liberal viewpoints."

Widespread Valuing of Collaboration across Disciplines

For students to get frequent exposure to collaboration and its benefits, faculty across the campus need to appreciate, value, and often employ collaboration in their courses. In our interviews, collaboration seemed to be a widespread mode of teaching and learning across disciplines, with perhaps humanities faculty speaking of it somewhat less often than faculty in other disciplines. Faculty especially pointed out how important collaboration will be in the students' future.

For example, when asked to pick one key feature that helps produce effective liberal arts education and that characterizes the experience of his freshman and sophomore students, psychology professor #1 responded,

> From my end the number one thing I focus on is collaborative assignments. I want students to realize that it is very rare that they will work in isolation. They will want to work with other people because different people have different strengths. They need to tap into others' strengths and their own strengths. So we do a lot of stuff with Myers Briggs [personality test] in my intro class, learning about different personality types. I want them to see the strengths of different personalities. For example, in the US many people see introversion as something to be cured. But why should that be so?

The professor alludes that introverts have strengths to contribute to collaborative work as much as extroverts do.

Faculty Views on the Benefits of Collaboration

Collaboration Enhances Overall Learning

Besides its utility in any career, another reason that faculty see collaboration as an important part of their pedagogy is that it enhances students' overall learning. Economics professor #2 has witnessed this when assigning students to work together in class to solve problems based on completed class readings that are difficult for any one student to solve by themselves. She says such assignments solve the problem of students complaining about others not contributing to group work equally.

She explains,

> When they only work in groups in class, they cannot complain about some people doing less work than others. The point of the team work I assign is to give them problems that are more difficult than what stu-

dents would be typically capable of solving alone—more applied problems. To solve the problem, they have to understand the basic concepts and have completed the readings individually before class. I do not teach those.

She continues to explain that in class, students first take a test on the readings individually, covering one to three chapters at a time. Right after that, they take the same test as a group. "That really shows them the value of a group," she says. "It clarifies ideas and shows them where they were wrong. They get feedback right away. This is the way Team Based Learning (TBL) pedagogy is structured."

At the beginning of her career, this professor did not assign this kind of group work in class because she did not trust that students would be capable of doing it well. "I felt that I needed to give a lecture on the things they now learn in groups," she says, and continues to point out that one of her biggest rewards from using TBL pedagogy has been the realization that students can understand much more than she expected and that "they have such great questions. If you let them do the readings themselves," she has found, "they have the tools to ask questions. They will be listening to learn the answer. Otherwise, if you give them those things in lecture only and then ask a question right away, they usually do not understand why you asked them the question."

When, in this way, independent learning is coupled with working with peers, students find they learn more, as reflected in one student's comment: "I learn a lot by going over the material with other students."

In turn, economics professor #1 uses student input in notes written on the board during class to enhance overall learning. He says he likes it when class notes include student work. "It is a problem if there is no student work in class notes," he stresses. "For instance, right now I have a student who is better in calculus than I will ever be. I want him to show the class how he does Lagrangean Multiplier. So I asked him to work that on the board. I like the idea of modeling; I think students can model for each other."

Psychology professor #2 uses group discussion in class to dialogue and brainstorm. In this process, she says, students acquire greater ownership of their work. She has seen that the enhanced learning from collaboration shows up in improved student work: "Students have to come to class with questions that are provocative and interesting," she says. "Then they talk about them. Collaboration is a way of forcing listening and a sensitivity to others' perspectives, a realization that we all stand on each other's shoulders." For these reasons she believes the quality of group projects "can be so much more" than the quality of an individual's work.

Collaboration Teaches Students to Teach Each Other

The importance of students learning from each other was stressed by several faculty. A physical education professor has gone so far as to give extra points in her class participation grade to students who help their classmates. The way she defines class participation is that "if a student feels comfortable with his or her personal skill, (s)he should turn around and help his or her neighbor." Thus in her class, class participation grade includes "self-learning and sharing that learning with others." Then, at the end of the semester, she asks students to identify the classmates that have been helpful to them.

The same principle is at work in science classes, where a biology professor emphasizes that students can learn much from each other and from teaching others. "I have argued for years that the greatest leadership opportunity a student can have on campus is to be a Supplemental Instructor (SI) or a lab teaching assistant in biology," she points out. "It is about the contribution that students make to the learning of other students." She asks her students, 'What do *you* see as the problem that your fellow students are having, and how can *you* help in that?'"

Student Views on Collaboration

As in the faculty interviews, the main aspect of student comments on collaborative assignments centered on how such assignments have taught them to work with others. This was reflected in comments such as the following: "It teaches you to compromise and be diplomatic," and, "During my freshman and sophomore years, we stressed working in groups. But what I learned has really helped me in business school. Now I know how to work with people and do well."

Another business school student sees the effects of a high level of collaboration in the first two years of college on her classmates, too: "A lot of our stuff in business school is group work, and I have noticed that my classmates [from freshman and sophomore years] are more willing to work with others. We know how to work with other people, no matter what background others come from or what the project is."

Students acknowledge that a part of the reason for this is how a small campus brings students into frequent contact with each other, how it minimizes "slacking off." One student said, "On a small campus, students feel pressure because if someone doesn't do their part of the project, you'll see them in the dining hall an hour later, and you can hammer them down." The same way, they said seeing other group members "in an hour or so" helped them be more diplomatic.

However, students also emphasized a sense of reliance on others that is forged by close peer-to-peer relationships that in their experience formed already during freshman orientation. One student spoke of trust between students on the small campus, something she has found wanting in a larger context. Trust undoubtedly makes teamwork easier. Another, senior, student said that already during her freshman year, "my friends and I held each other accountable."

Teaching Leadership

When a campus utilizes collaboration extensively—both in academic and nonacademic contexts—it is easier to teach leadership as well. A professor teaching a Foundations of Leadership class explains how she teaches leadership in her class: "I first have them read definitions of leadership by different researchers. They get different perspectives, noticing that the definition of leadership begins to coalesce around the idea that leaders today *are* more collaborative."

She points out that she has found it more useful to lead and guide her students, instead of telling them, "You should think about leadership in this way." She explains, "That way, *they* start to assert that leadership should be collaborative." The Dean for Campus Life similarly explains that student leadership programs operate on the premise that "we aim for students to be self-aware, to know who they are, what their strengths are, how to develop these skills, *how to work with other people* who bring different skill sets and viewpoints, and how to solve ethical problems collaboratively" (emphasis added). Both in-class collaborative assignments and extracurricular leadership development thus coalesce around the idea that people should work together for the common good.

Another strategy of the professor teaching the Foundations of Leadership class is to emphasize to the students the importance of "small acts of leadership," and the consequences of both good and bad leadership. She describes this strategy: "We talk about how ordinary people can do amazing things. We talk about Rosa Parks, Nelson Mandela, and others. I tell the students that it is an act of leadership if your friends are putting someone down, and you say, 'Hey, that is not right!'" She says that at the end of the semester she sees more students as potential leaders.

She wants the students to see that "bad leadership is very costly (because it leads to a decline in productivity—as good workers leave the organization). Also, being a good leader is the right thing to do. So," she emphasizes, "leadership deals both with efficiency and ethical considerations."

Learning Leadership

The interviewed students attested to the ample opportunities and good consequences that being involved in leadership and collaboration during their freshman and sophomore years had for them. Collaboration was so common that, as one student put it, "Regardless of whether you were in a certain leadership position or not, you always had a chance to be a leader in some way."

She also said that collaboration/involvement/leadership taught her to care. The consequence of that for her and most of her classmates from freshman and sophomore years who too were actively involved has been that in their junior and senior years, they are "in a certain club or organization because they care about it, not because they want it on their resume." She says that some of her fellow students in junior and senior years have been "almost surprised by how much effort I put into my extracurriculars. I do it because I care."

Students also said that during their freshman-year leadership training, they learned teamwork. "That's what leadership is," one person said, continuing, "We learn that leadership is stepping back when you need to, encouraging other people when you see that they have a better plan." Another person described her sophomore-year experience in cofacilitating a class this way: "I loved reading the papers that kids would submit. I really learned how to facilitate discussion, which I continue to do. I love asking questions and encouraging others to discuss." Serving in a leadership position thus taught students how to operate and cooperate with others.

Both collaborative assignments and leadership development are undoubtedly easier to manage and "enforce" in a small context. But it is not automatic that a spirit of collaboration and trust arises among students, especially in a highly diverse community. In the interviews, students gave credit both to a sense of community and the opportunities they had in their freshman and sophomore years. The opportunities to develop one's leadership skills are certainly greater if there is a close collaboration between academic and student life. Campuses with a clearer division between student life and academics offer perhaps a narrower experience of leadership on campus.

A small campus helps students stay in more frequent contact with each other. Yet it still faces the challenge of creating and nurturing relevant opportunities that foster cooperation and the development of needed skills. It also has to nurture a culture of active participation. Due to the multiple opportunities afforded to the students we interviewed, many students developed a love of involvement and engagement, experiences linked to leadership and collaboration. In the words of one student, "I loved being able to be an active part of the campus so easily, do my job as a life guard and SI, and be a PAL [peer assistant leader] at the same time." Another said she "got to do so many random things," such as work with alumni and lead campus tours.

Of course, the downside of multiple opportunities, the spirit of involvement, and a small campus is that sometimes, students may overextend themselves and feel that they "have to be a part of everything," or "the 'super student complex,'" as yet another student put it. Some find it hard to balance their coursework and extracurricular activities, challenging the campus to promote a healthy level of engagement. When the appreciation of involvement and collaboration is coupled with high academic expectations, some students may feel overwhelmed, potentially leading to experiences like the exhaustion and sleep deprivation mentioned in chapter 1.

Having addressed collaborative assignments, "collaborative leadership," and the impact that collaboration has on the individual, we get to the issue of the larger purposes and means of education. Collaboration in class and in student organizations leads us to the topic of collaboration for the good of the surrounding community.

The next chapter will discuss service learning and community-based learning—a HIP that speaks to teaching the whole student and connects learning to the broader life. It will address the idea of faculty being mindful of both the soul and the spirit of their students when teaching, not only their mind. It can be argued that education is of highest impact when it shapes all parts of a person, has lasting behavioral consequences, and causes students to be active in their community and in the world.

NOTES

1. Students' development in extracurricular contexts will also be discussed in the next chapter.

2. Panitz provides a brief history of each of the terms "cooperative" and "collaborative" learning and distinguishes their development in different educational environments (pp. 5–8).

3. Pascarella, E. T., Ethington, D., & Smart, J. (1988). The influence of college on humanitarian/civic involvement values. *Journal of Higher Education, 59*, 412–37.

4. Referencing Astin, H. S., & Leland, C. (1991). *Women of influence, women of vision: A cross-generational study of leaders and social change*. San Francisco, CA: Jossey-Bass; Cress, C. M., Astin, H. S., Zimmerman-Oster, K., & Burkhardt, J. C. (2001). Developmental outcomes of college students' involvement in leadership activities. *Journal of College Student Development, 42*, 15–27; Komives, S. R., Lucas, N., & McMahon, T. R. (2006). *Exploring leadership: For college students who want to make a difference*. San Francisco, CA: Jossey-Bass.

SIX

Teaching the Whole Student: Taking Learning into the Realm of Experience

Service learning and community-based learning constitute another high-impact practice that shares characteristics with many other HIPs already mentioned. For example, serving in the community usually involves students working with each other, and, certainly, active learning. Another name for it is "experiential learning"—learning that occurs when classroom concepts are "experienced" in practice in the community, and when, in turn, students reflect upon the lessons learned in the community when they are back in the classroom.

While community-based learning is the less precisely defined of the two, service learning is understood as a "*credit-bearing* educational experience in which students participate in an organized service activity that meets identified community needs" (Bringle & Hatcher, 1996[1] cited in Zlotkowski, 1998, p. xiv; emphasis added). It thus differs from extracurricular volunteering in that it takes place as part of a course, being intimately tied to the course's learning objectives (ibid).

In this chapter, we discuss service learning and community-based learning as part of a bigger aim of and approach to education. That is, we consider that teaching the "whole student"—extending learning to one's broader life and community—of which service learning and community-based learning are a part, is a high-impact approach to teaching. It includes taking learning into the realm of experience, and into realms of self other than just the intellectual or cognitive.

In addition to service, the affected dimensions of life in teaching the whole student are spirituality, the affective domain, and ethics. Each of these taps into or calls upon the experiential dimension of the human experience. In many cases, these can occur in the classroom, but they very often involve exploration of relationships with fellow students out of the

59

class, and relationships with those outside the immediate campus community. As we offer students the opportunity to put into practice or "experience" learning, we increase the pedagogical possibilities, the contexts within which learning may occur, and the effectiveness of learning.

This chapter first reviews some past studies on and insights from teaching the whole student, experiential learning, and service learning, and then outlines how faculty and students have utilized and experienced these practices.

PAST STUDIES AND PRACTICES IN TEACHING THE WHOLE STUDENT

The idea that teaching should extend to students' affective and even spiritual domains relate to an understanding that the goals of education should not be intellectual only. As Boyer recounts, the early American college had as one of its purposes to "educate the whole person"(1987, p. 177). In contrast, since the early to mid-twentieth century, the connection between education, faith, and soul has been loosened (ibid).

Recently, Zajonc (in Palmer & Zajonc, 2010) and Astin et al. (2011) have continued to lament something Boyer identified in the late 1980s: college education lacks relevance to students' lives. "[U]ndergraduates find it difficult to see patterns in their courses and to relate what they learn to life," as Boyer puts it (1987, p. 3).

To address this, Palmer and Zajonc (2010) have argued for the inclusion of the whole student in education, a perspective they mainly refer to as "integrative education," or "the whole human being in community" (p. 16). In the foreword to the authors' book, Nepo calls this "holistic education" (p. vii). It encompasses the mind, heart, and spirit, and emphasizes a "relational view of reality," whether among or within the various disciplines, the learner him/herself, or between individuals and the community (Zajonc in ibid, p. 81).

We discuss the individual's role in the community more below. Zajonc argues that in their attempt to "make [themselves] over into a 'science,'" most disciplines have suffered from "objectification and disconnection" (p. 81). As a result, "the education of the whole human being in community and the cultivation of his or her humanity seem to be increasingly forgotten for the sake of scientific simplification" (ibid, pp. 81–82).

Arguing against such simplification, Zajonc advocates for an "undivided life," in which education and the rest of one's life are not disconnected from purpose and meaning (Palmer & Zajonc, 2010, p. 56). Himself a physicist, he urges scientific fields to give "far more attention" to lived experience, connection, and complexity (p. 82). Indeed, part of teaching the whole student is to help students see how their education relates to their personal lives and futures.

In reviewing hundreds of studies, Pascarella and Terenzini (1991) found that "where stronger and clearer links can be forged between students' lives and course content skills, student engagement and change are likely to follow" (p. 652). This is confirmed by student accounts: in his study analyzing interviews of more than 1,600 undergraduates, Light (2001) found that for students, the "faculty members who had an especially big impact [on students' thinking and lives] are those who helped students make connections between a serious curriculum, on the one hand, and the students' personal lives, values, and experiences, on the other" (p. 110).

A student whom Light quotes, argues that connecting classroom material to students' lives helps one learn better: faculty who invite students "to make connections between abstract ideas and their own real lives" produce learning that "transcends what I would call purely academic learning, and is really seared into our consciousness" (ibid, p. 113).

One way in which courses can relate to students' lives and futures, as Bok (2006), argues, is by providing an increased understanding of vocational choices—courses that do not need to be narrowly "professional," but ones that could involve moral/ethical reasoning vis-à-vis potential occupations. That way students would be exposed to the ethical issues of, for example, the medical practice—something that may help them think about how they would feel about being in that profession.

Vocational choice and understanding of purpose are important because, as Zajonc puts it, "Long after they forget the content they learned, *who they have become* will endure and determine much of the character and quality of their contribution to society and the personal satisfaction they take in life" (Palmer & Zajonc, 2010, p. 102, emphasis added).

Vocation relates closely to meaning and purpose, which in turn relates to spirituality. While some think that spirituality has no place in academic inquiry, one can argue, as Astin et al. (2011) do, that education should help equip students to deal both with the outside world and students' inner lives. Palmer stresses that "[r]eligion and spirituality are among the major drivers of contemporary life (Palmer & Zajonc, 2010, p. 47)," and Astin et al. list some common facets of contemporary life the solving of which requires more than technical knowledge: divorce, substance abuse, wars, and so on.

They also remind us that "colleges and universities are already deeply involved" in issues that pertain to "spiritual" and personal matters such as aspirations, dreams, values, and beliefs, through, for example, academic advising and residential life (p. 6). Yet these matters do not usually receive explicit attention. Rather, as Astin et al. put it, higher education "has increasingly come to neglect its students' 'inner' development," including emotional maturity, moral development, spirituality, and self-understanding (ibid, p. 2).

One could point out that to approach education through contemplation and even spirituality is in accord with a number of educational movements focusing on holistic development, such as the Teaching the Whole Child Movement in elementary education and Developing the Whole Student in university education.

How, specifically, can institutions ensure that they instruct students with such a wider set of goals and purposes? In many institutions, the connection between the various dimensions of self has been perhaps most explicitly cultivated in student affairs, in which the "the development of the whole person constitutes the core function of the student affairs profession" (Braxton, 2009, p. 573).

But certainly faculty, too, can incorporate these aspects into their teaching. According to Quinlan (2011), "[a] key ingredient is the use of active pedagogies such as service learning, problem-based learning and discussion of moral dilemmas in the discipline" (p. 3). Palmer says that "[d]oing integrative education well depends on our capacity to hold a paradox: we must open free space for the unpredictable *and* enforce an educative order" (Palmer & Zajonc, 2010, p. 39). Opening such free space can entail, for example, the use of inquiry-guided learning. As described in chapter 3, inquiry classes aim to allow for a more open-ended outcome for course projects and questions.

Uhl (2011) elaborates on another way: teachers could begin to reconnect theories, facts, and knowledge to a number of other human capabilities that are vital to an integrated and more complete understanding. His thought is to revitalize traditional subject-focused learning with a broader focus on a new set of three Rs—Relationship with Self, Relationship with Other, and Relationship with Earth. He urges educators to be creative in designing courses that will engage students' feelings, ethics, as well as the more complex cognitive processes.

One example that Uhl provides in his chapter on bringing emotions into the learning process deals with the acknowledgment of negative feelings in the classroom. He explains how his colleague Dana Stuchul conducts a "fear" exercise in order to make students more aware of the negative power of this feeling, if left unacknowledged. In this exercise, Stuchul randomly selects seven students at the beginning of class to come to the front of the class to explain what the current or previous lesson involved. When the first surprised student falters even slightly, Stuchul feigns a wince and moves to the next student.

Before very long, all the students in the room become very tense, as those selected to come to the front begin to feel the teacher's displeasure in a number of ways. Drama over. Afterward, students are delighted when they find this was a mock exercise, designed to bring to their awareness how teaching in this way fosters little learning and a tidal wave of fear. Working against this kind of environment, both Stuchul and Uhl foster awareness of the emotions that can or should be present in the classroom setting, but are neglected all too often.

PAST STUDIES, PRACTICES, AND TRENDS IN EXPERIENTIAL LEARNING, SERVICE LEARNING

Emotions, connection to the broader community, spirituality . . . these aspects of teaching the whole student are often present perhaps most powerfully when students work directly with community members. The emphasis thus shifts from the inner lives of students, and in general the students themselves, to the broader context in which students live. Experiential-, service-, and community-based learning provide this context.

Service in the community is one form of experiential learning; others are undergraduate research, internships, and off-campus courses, in all of which learning rests on the assumption that students learn best by doing. While hands-on activity is able to produce greater learning than mere listening, note-taking, or even discussion, service-learning experiences also point students to the importance of "something other than themselves" (Boyer, 1987, p. 68).

Boyer's argument in favor of "something other than oneself" is worth quoting in full:

> Individuals should become empowered to live productive, independent lives. They also should be helped to go beyond private interests and place their own lives in larger context. When the observant Frenchman Alexis de Tocqueville visited the United States in the 1830s, he warned that "as individualism grows, people forget their ancestors and form the habit of thinking of themselves in isolation and imagine their whole destiny is in their hands." To counter this cultural disintegration, Tocqueville argued, "Citizens must turn from the private inlets and occasionally take a look at something other than themselves"[2] (Boyer, 1987, p. 68).

The goal of service activities in particular, Boyer continues, is "to help students see that they are not only autonomous individuals but also members of a larger community to which they are accountable" (ibid, p. 218). Service also helps "channel knowledge to humane ends" and foster commitment—not just competence (ibid, p. 219). These are increasingly accepted aims of higher education: "Since the early 1990s, momentum has been building toward the creation of a far more socially engaged academy" (Zlotkowski, 2005, p. 360).

There are those who would link service learning to broader democracy (as originally done by John Dewey). Densmore (2000), for example, sums up the arguments of other studies concerning the benefit of service to society: when students are engaged in service, "[t]he quality of democracy will be enhanced because individual students will assume a measure of social responsibility" (p. 49). Student participation in service activities may therefore help counter the growth in citizen apathy and isolationism, about which Bok (2006) and (Putnam, 1995; 2000), respectively, have written.[3]

The roots of service learning can be found in the 1960s when during the Kennedy years the Peace Corps was first envisioned (Jacoby, 1996). In a similar spirit, the idea of giving to the surrounding community became the core idea of many university-run community service programs—but as the decade faded, so did the university-sponsored service programs (ibid). Kendall and associates (1990) offer three reasons for their failure: lack of integration into the actual mission of each institution, an almost condescending paternalistic approach to "helping others," and, there was no mechanism for assuring that students actually learned.

In the mid-1980s, community service programs were renewed, and out of this second wave of programs the idea to connect the service to student learning gained more traction. New programs began to incorporate the lessons of the first generation of programs and began to set up partnerships that aligned with the newly voiced mission of the institution, while academics began to seek and develop ways to develop student learning in the service projects. The idea to have students share and write about their experiences upon reflection gained prominence. As the two sides of the equation became more recognized—service *and* learning—the scholarly literature on service learning grew exponentially.

There is also a vast literature on the features that help make service learning successful. Below is an outline. For service learning to benefit both students and the community, commonly mentioned requirements are that service learning complements and deepens students' understanding of course material, that there is true partnership between the college and the community, and that service addresses real problems in the community (Brownell & Swaner, 2009; Densmore, 2000; O'Grady, 2000; Rosenberger, 2000).

This true partnership between the college and the community requires mutuality and reciprocity (Rosenberger, 2000), instead of a paternalistic attitude (O'Grady, 2000). O'Grady's (2000) book puts together a powerful argument in favor of combining service learning with multicultural education, stating that service learning must address the "complexity of racial and cultural difference" that is often present in the service context (O'Grady, 2000, xiv). Besides for ethical reasons, this should be done, the authors argue, because "multicultural education is truly transformative for students only when it includes a community action component, and likewise, service learning is truly a catalyst for change only when it is done from a multicultural and socially just perspective" (ibid, xv).

That service learning addresses real problems in the community requires an understanding of the social issues involved, and policies affecting those issues. As O'Grady puts it, "Responding to individual human needs is important, but if the social policies that create these needs [are] not also understood and addressed, then the cycle of dependence remains" (2000, p. 13).

In line with this, Langseth (2000) argues that *if* service learning aims to promote "longer range community change" (p. 251), what is required is "significant knowledge about the people we are working with," "strategic intentionality" (p. 254), and making relationship building, not "finding the 'right' programmatic 'fix,'" one's first priority (p. 249). This builds trust. With these conditions, allotting enough service hours, adequate monitoring of activities in the field (Brownell & Swaner, 2009), and structured and frequent reflection (ibid; Boyer, 1987; Zlotkowski, 2005), service learning provides an opportunity to "think critically and comprehensively about human issues that are basic to the quality of human life" (O'Grady, 2000, p. xiv).

Among both those who give and those who receive the service, service learning then ideally develops the ability to "view the world from multiple perspectives" (ibid, p. xiv). It also develops "people who are participants in inquiry, who know how to ask the right questions, who understand the process by which public policy is shaped [refer back to 'good teaching' characterized in chapter 3], and are prepared to make informed, discriminating judgments on questions that affect the future" (Boyer, 1987, p. 280).

The challenge confronted by faculty teaching the whole student as well as service learning is: how can rigorous content standards be maintained and even extended all the while inviting students' broader expressions and involvement in and beyond the classroom in a more fully human sense? The conviction held by many is that involving more of the human being in the learning process leads both to better learning and better citizens.

EXAMPLES OF TEACHING THE WHOLE STUDENT AND EXPERIENTIAL LEARNING

Faculty, staff, and student interviews revealed additional conditions that help address the whole student and facilitate experiential learning. For example, on a smaller campus and in general when students and faculty are used to working closely together, it is easier to forge the kinds of relationships between students, faculty, and staff in which more personal give and take is possible and likely. Teaching the whole student and experiential learning also require opportunities and resources to apply course content in students' lives and in the community.

Applicability of Courses to Students' Lives

Several faculty emphasized the importance of the applicability of their teaching to students' lives, a two-way interaction between students' lives and the faculty member's teaching. For example, a psychology professor (psychology professor #1) put it in the following way: "Central to my mission as a teacher . . . is meaning making: how students see the relevance of my discipline to their daily lives. That is *the* most important factor to me. If they leave my Theories of Personalities class with the names of the great theorists and some theories but do not see how those theories play out in their lives and the lives of others, then I have failed to help them get something out of the course."

She adds, "I think that engagement in substantive ways—through conversation, writing, service learning—is the best tool for meaning making," and continues further: "I used to believe that when students tried to connect material to their personal lives, that was 'nuisance material.' I was a scientist and I wanted them to know what we know. . . . When students said, 'I don't care what the textbook says; this is my experience,' that used to be hard for me to accept. But now that is what I *want* to hear."

This is because her primary concern has shifted from course content—things to be covered—to students' development as people. As incoming students' credentials at her institution have improved year after year, she knows that she currently has "the brightest students" she has ever had. Yet her concern is, "Are they going to be good people? Are they going to find meaning, joy, purpose? Are they going to be taking care of each other?" She now focuses on those in her teaching.

Faculty also seek to make their teaching applicable to students' lives on campus. In her leadership class, psychology professor #2 explains, one of the most meaningful assignments has been when she asked students to work in teams to identify an area on campus that they felt needed improvement and then lead efforts in that area to affect change. She is clearly proud of her students when she shares, "They had to contact the right people and identify a workable strategy. They were forced to be very constructive." She said the students realized it is not easy to change things but also that it is possible if one does it wisely.

Campus problem solving is certainly one way to connect course material to students' lives. Another is through a connection to "current affairs," as one student put it. This student praised a biology professor who taught her students about cancer research. "We got to look at cancer cells," the student explains. "It became a practical thing; it wasn't just something in a text book. . . . I'm not a science person at all, but after taking that class, I thought, 'Wow,' I could actually understand science."

Establishing relevance and applying material to students' lives was clearly a theme that students too appreciated in their course content.

Another student reminisced about another biology professor for a similar reason: "She explained how we learn things and how we apply them to real life and to situations we haven't learned in class. She sat us down and told us, 'This is how you learn.' By doing that, she helped us a lot. . . . With her, we were 'seeing' the importance of course material; we were feeling it. It's the experience that makes the knowledge more embedded. That way, it is not superficial learning."

This was echoed among students and faculty alike, across the disciplines. In chemistry, a professor describes her experience in involving students in the making of bio-fuel, saying it was a very powerful learning experience. What made it such?

> It was the fact that our class was actually making something that could be used by someone in a way that was important to the world. This assignment is something I know they still think about today. We really investigated what bio-fuels are, why they are necessary, and what is the need for them. This is not something you normally do in an organic chemistry class. It changed the framework under which we all operate. All of a sudden, we were doing something that could benefit others. . . . It was the applicability of the things they were doing.

Faculty also stressed student responsibility in applying their learning to good ends, and continuing to do that after they graduate. A sociology professor describes his philosophy that he shares when meeting with families of prospective students:

> I tell them we will set the occasion to develop students' skills that are consistent with life as an adult. That is the call of a college. I do not go into explaining the differences in lifetime earnings of people with a high-school degree and a college degree. What I talk about is that students will be called upon to produce something of value to their employer. I also share things like the fact that we have some of the lowest voting rates in the world.

Teaching to the Soul and Spirit, Not Only the Mind

In the same vein, many faculty stressed the wider context of students as persons—not only their intellectual capacity. For example, citing Palmer (and Zajonc [2010]), a political science professor emphasizes how important it is to him that his teaching nurtures not only the mind but also the spirit—that students would not leave their emotions and beliefs out of the learning process.

He says he never requires students to share their emotions or beliefs but that he invites them to do so, finding that: "Some people will never speak up about their private matters, and I do not press them to express those in class, whether they are religious, cultural, or whatever. But some students will volunteer. And I encourage all of them to think about it. That should be part of their gaining of knowledge." He finds that some students need to be directed away from the subject matter specifically to what the issue means to them. In such cases, he encourages students by saying that if anything in their learning triggers a memory, "from whatever the source, reason or emotion, they should be drawing from that."

There are those students for whom connecting the subject matter to their lives is the best part of the class. The professor describes, "Some people just start pouring their hearts out, without me even asking for it," but quickly adds that he does not want students to "deliver things in an emotional way." Yet he does want them "to draw from those aspects of life."

This is the call about which some faculty feel very strongly, and relates to the emotional attachment with the subject matter mentioned as an effective teaching strategy in chapter 3. Psychology professor #1 references and agrees with Astin et al. (2011) in that despite the expressed desire by students to tap into and learn about the spiritual, most universities do not really address this dimension. "We say that we teach the whole person," she says, "but we do not. If you look at the mission statements of almost all universities and colleges, they say that they are doing that, but when you look at the curricula, those things are not reflected. The academia is so frightened of teaching or encountering the heart, the spirit."

Experiential Learning

Community service/service learning may be one way that students naturally come into contact with the emotional, the spiritual, and the beliefs they hold both of themselves and others, as they serve, often, people who are very different from themselves. An interviewed faculty member stressed that it was service learning that really allowed her to see how students make meaning of life and what they learn. "That is when I began slowly moving away from the podium," she said.

Service learning can also offer ways to implement an inquiry-driven curriculum more effectively, practically, and naturally than classroom discussion alone can. As a professor explains: "We have seen students engage in the kind of questioning in which we want to see them engage *on the basis of their experience in the community.*" Thus service-learning courses can support not only the teaching of the whole student but also the teaching of inquiry.

While experiential learning courses do not necessarily provide answers to students' questions, they *can* help students ask better questions. Also, many interviewed students reported that their service activities were some of the most impactful part of their freshman and sophomore years. "The campus culture often considered non-class-related activities as part of learning," a student described. "Many of us engaged in service outside of class because it complemented our education."

This student is talking about how out-of-class volunteering can complement learning that takes place in courses, whether the courses are service-learning courses or more traditional ones. Volunteering—another form of experiential learning—can be an important part of applying classroom learning, as almost half of all students on four-year campuses volunteer during their college years (Bok, 2006).

The students talked about what they had learned through their community-service experiences. The courses helped many of them clarify or confirm their career interests (for example, one student realized he did not want to become a doctor but found another way to serve in the medical field) and connect students with each other. The director of student development adds that she has seen students develop self-confidence and a love for service; the service experiences have also often helped students make connections between classes.

When such opportunities are given to freshmen, the director of student development continues, the boost to students' self-confidence is even greater. With freshmen normally "at the bottom of the pecking order," they feel a sense of appreciation through their service positions. This applies to opportunities both for leadership roles and community service, which are often one and the same thing. Service opportunities support sophomores' self-confidence and leadership development as well because sophomores are the natural leaders on a two-year campus.

Faculty and staff also pointed to a smooth cooperation between academics and campus life in facilitating opportunities and student growth, not only in service learning but in general. When academics and campus life work together as a true partnership, it helps improve communication and logistics between faculty, students, staff, and personnel at service placements. "It takes a lot of time to build the community partnerships and work through the logistics," the director of student development says. "We need to be responsible to what the community needs."

She points out that one way to identify what the community needs is by browsing through the local newspapers to see what community issues the papers report. She used this method when she learned, for example, that many local veterans are not receiving the benefits for which they are eligible. She then tried to figure out how students could help with that.

Yet there are still challenges in ensuring the intentionality and match between course goals and the service activity, identifying services opportunities in some areas—for example, economics—and integrating international students fully into the service experience. For international students, community service often means interacting with agencies and cultures that are foreign to them; serving in a second language poses an additional challenge. On the other hand, the presence of international students can help break down barriers among students and with different segments of the surrounding community.

Therefore, a diverse student body contributes to the teaching of the whole student and experiential learning by increasing the perspectives and approaches to which students will be exposed. It can also counter the criticism leveled at the demographic imbalance often involved in community engagement, in that a sizeable group of international (and other "minority") students ensures that service is no longer given primarily by white American students to members of other groups.

Diversity can also contribute to the incorporation of "spirituality" in teaching, in that "spiritual qualities" as a whole are often "enhanced when undergraduates are provided with opportunities to experience multiple perspectives and diverse peoples" (Astin et al., 2011, p. 137). The next chapter demonstrates further how exposure to student diversity and diverse perspectives can enhance student learning, and what implications diversity has for teaching.

NOTES

1. Bringle, R. G., & Hatcher, J. A. (1996). Implementing service-learning in higher education. *Journal of Higher Education, 67*(2), 221–239.
2. De Tocqueville, A. (1835). *Democracy in America*. In Mayer, J. P. (Ed.). (1969), Garden City, NY: Doubleday, pp. 508, 510.
3. Other benefits of service learning were listed in the Preface.

SEVEN

Putting HIPs in Context: (Interactions with) Diversity

The landscape of higher education seems to present a unique formative issue every two or three years. As listed in an American Association of State Colleges and Schools Policy Report published in 2013, today's defining issues include improving institutional performance, student college readiness, online education (MOOCs), tuition prices, for-profit colleges, and gun control on college campuses, among others (Hurley et al., 2013).

Significantly, however, one key topic, the increasing diversity of the student population, is missing, perhaps because it has received quite a lot of attention for more than two decades. Yet the challenges have not gone away—neither has the need for colleges to understand just how to take advantage of increasing levels and types of diversity, helping students benefit from it.

This chapter discusses how faculty and staff can engage students to successfully interact with and learn from "diversity"—whether the concept refers to diversity of people or of issues. The Association of American Colleges and Universities (AAC&U) emphasizes the learning potential in courses that incorporate diverse views, while the Wabash National Study additionally highlights the importance of students' "diversity interactions" with peers and others. Both fall under the topic of interest in this chapter.

Diversity interactions are interactions that students have with those on and off campus who are culturally/racially different from them and/or who come from different socioeconomic backgrounds or hold different religious and/or political views. This is an important issue for the overall understanding of the operation of high-impact educational practices, as diversity represents, besides an HIP in its own right, the context in which

71

all other HIPs will *increasingly* be taking place. The shares of both minorities and international students nationwide are increasing.[1]

Below, after reviewing current knowledge about diversity on college campuses, this chapter discusses how faculty (and staff) should handle and take advantage of diversity, and how students view this issue.

THE NEED FOR DIVERSITY AND THE ROLE OF A COLLEGE

Analysts and practitioners have long argued that to improve intergroup communication, structural diversity is not enough. Neither does structural diversity necessarily increase learning. Yet it is necessary that a campus has a certain level of representation from each demographic group — not yet a reality everywhere. Journalist Kimberly Hefling of the *Huffington Post* reported in September 2013: "The Obama administration told colleges and universities [that] they can continue to use admissions to increase diversity among their students, even in the wake of a Supreme Court ruling that could potentially open the door to more challenges."

Her quote from the administration's letter to schools reminds us that one of the first meanings of developing a "diverse campus" still refers to a racially diverse campus: "Racially diverse educational environments help to prepare students to succeed in our increasingly diverse nation." At the beginning of 2014, the same administration also called for increasing economic diversity (Song, 2014). Besides race and class, religious diversity is of relevance on campuses, as is more recently the diversity of nationalities. In fact, in Light's (2001) study, students mentioned religious diversity as the aspect of diversity that most enhanced their learning in college — and this learning took mostly place outside of class.

Besides ensuring enough structural diversity, campuses need to know how to help students learn from diversity. The challenge is how to achieve diversity "while improving the social and learning environments for students" (Hurtado et. al, 1999, p. 2). To improve campus climate for racial diversity means each of the following must be studied and addressed in meaningful ways: historical patterns of exclusion, current beliefs and attitudes, and institutional values and practices — all intertwining to create the complexities of campus culture.

An understanding and preparedness to address these is a prerequisite for all on campus to benefit from diversity. Understanding the impact of institutional values, practices, and emphases is important because otherwise the presence of diverse groups on campus can actually hinder learning, as Light's (2001) study reveals. Light describes a situation in which students of vastly different skills and work habits took classes together, but did not share, for example, basic English language skills nor assumptions about working hard toward their degree.

This led to the following conclusion, as pointed out by the students Light interviewed:

> [H]ow well ethnic and racial diversity actually enhances learning depends largely on how well a college builds on, capitalizes on, and proactively strengthens this basic assumption. They say that if this assumption of certain shared values is undercut by campus culture, or faculty members, or college leadership, or even the leaders of student organizations, then positive educational benefits may not flow from diversity of ethnic and racial backgrounds. The risk of awkwardness may destroy learning (p. 133).

Therefore, while it is important for colleges to communicate "how diversity is central to education" (Hurtado et al., 1999, p. 4), they must also emphasize strong work ethic, high academic standards, and other expectations that set the tone for coursework and the educational experience in general.

For students to learn from diversity also requires that colleges increase interaction between various groups (Hurtado et al., 1999; King et al., 2011). Using the language of Allport's (1954) seminal work on group dynamics, King, Baxter Magolda, and Massé (2011) write about the conditions needed for intergroup contact to be positive:

> College campuses that foster interaction across difference can create a learning environment that promotes the five conditions related to positive intergroup relations—members have equal group status, parties are engaged in a cooperative effort, effort is in the service of a common goal, contact is officially sanctioned by institutional authorities, and friendship potential is present—in order to decrease latent intergroup anxiety (p. 482).

Still, even with these conditions present, group dynamics can sometimes be negative. The above authors lament that often, diversity education focuses on challenging students, yet educators should also help students to *make meaning from their experiences with diversity* to prevent students from getting "stuck." The authors thus "advocate *discomfort with support* as a means to promote students' intercultural maturity" (ibid, pp. 482-83; emphasis added). While facilitating discomfort sounds negative, discomfort can actually be good because it can enable growth (Ibid).

Moving students from early to full(er) intercultural maturity should be done step by step. This involves "[i]ncreas[ing] students' awareness and understanding of diverse interactions and their effects" (ibid, p. 483). Colleges should therefore *both* raise awareness about diversity and its benefits, *and* help students interact with diverse others and make meaning from those interactions.

Furthermore, colleges can help students learn empathy. This can be done, for example, by assigning students readings about the experiences of a disadvantaged group that has suffered discrimination, and then asking students to write about how the persons depicted in the story (may have) felt and how their situation could be improved (Stephan & Finlay, 1999).

There is much need for colleges to help students grow in intercultural maturity. Many students come to college from homogeneous backgrounds. According to Jones (2005), who references Orfield and Yun (1999),[2] there is now actually more segregation at the K–12 level than there was in the 1970s. Consequently, only in college do many students interact for the first time personally with students from different racial, cultural, or religious backgrounds, or with students with different values or political views.

Jones continues to describe how diversity is often difficult for students to handle:

> Today's college students appear to live in a world where they perceive little common ground, environments where traditional student organizations, clubs, and activities do not meet their needs for affiliation and identity. Students, rightly or wrongly, perceive that they have little in common with students from other cultures or ethnic groups, and they see themselves, regardless of affiliation groups, as victims of some other group's perceived advantages (p. 143).

Because of this lack of perceived common ground, Jones emphasizes, "Successful first-year student campus climate initiatives must stress the importance of inclusion in all organized student associations" (ibid, p. 144). Student clubs and other groups should not be based on members' race or background, and in general, such factors should play no role in the treatment of students in any facet of campus activity (Light, 2001).

Finally, the integration of international students in particular is a challenge that campuses face as their international student populations increase. This involves understanding the vastly different educational standards and cultures that various countries have. According to the *US News & World Report*, in the 2011–2012 academic year, a 6 percent increase in accepted international students across the United States set a historical record for increase, with international undergraduate students surpassing international graduate student numbers for the first time in twelve years (Smith-Barrow, 2014).

While the national average for international students by institution hovers around 5 percent, an increasing number of state schools, liberal arts colleges, and research institutions are admitting dramatically higher numbers. Such changes undoubtedly affect campus dynamics, with norms for engagement not being the same for students from different backgrounds.

For example, in his study of engagement at Australian universities, Edwards (2008) found that international students were more active than domestic students in certain types of activities — similar to the situation in

American colleges. These include learning in a community/group, working with other students during class, and studying a foreign language. Conversely, resident (Australian) students reported greater involvement in a somewhat different set of academic and student life activities, some of which may be true of American students at American universities as well—for example, asking questions in class, discussing ideas from classes with others, and being engaged in community service (ibid).

The different norms, experiences, and expectations held by students from different countries regarding both academics and involvement in various activities may require faculty and staff to modify their pedagogies and practices to draw in and benefit all students, as well as to take advantage of what students from different backgrounds bring to the table.

STUDENTS' ROLE

Yet constructive diversity encounters depend not only on the school (context) but also on the individual students involved. One factor is students' background. Those who have interacted with others across racial lines in high school are also more likely to do so in college. And those who interact with diverse peers more often are also more likely to have positive interactions—compared to those who interact with them less (Locks et al., 2008).

Second, King and colleagues (2011) point out that what and how a person learns from interaction with others depends upon the extent to which (s)he is "self-authored" (p. 471). This refers to the student's ability/readiness/inclination to make decisions based on internal processing, as opposed to relying on external sources (ibid). In her study of the sophomore year, Schaller (2005) echoes the importance of students learning to rely on their own internal voice, instead of authority figures. This refers to choosing one's major as well. "Active learning suggests not simply an external activity but an internal process" (ibid, p. 22).

Citing other sources, King, Baxter Magolda, and Massé (2011) continue, "The many college students who rely on external sources . . . often report being overwhelmed in situations that require independent judgment, taking a stand, and an understanding of life complexities (e.g., disciplinary, social) that cannot be reduced to dichotomies" (pp. 471–72).

A third way in which the benefit from diversity interactions depends on the student is highlighted by a student interviewed in Light's (2001) study. The student says, "Learning from diversity depends so much on being a reflective student" (p. 145). A person who reflects on his or her experiences can make better sense of and learn from those experiences.

In sum, how much diversity benefits students depends, first, on an individual student's conditioning and experiences regarding diversity (determining how they will respond to it), and second, on how the college handles and capitalizes on diversity (how the college responds to it), provided that there is enough structural diversity to begin with.

BENEFITS OF DIVERSITY

The literature identifies several benefits that students may reap from exposure to and interaction with diverse others. The benefits accrue both from academic contexts (faculty introducing diverse topics as well as diverse students bringing different perspectives to class) and interpersonal encounters between students. Students often find the latter more impactful (Light, 2001).

For example, diversity interactions can have a positive effect on cognitive growth due to the fact that diverse perspectives bring "discontinuity and discrepancy" to the lives of students who mostly come to college from segregated environments (Gurin et al., 2002, p. 335). A positive effect on students is also due to an increase in "academic self-confidence" (Laird, 2005).

In Light's (2001) study, a student talked about this confidence: growing up in an area with very few students of his racial/ethnic group going on to achieve at high levels, he found that at Harvard, there were many high-achieving, ambitious individuals like him. This strengthened his confidence in who he was. For him, the most important "diversity" he found at his college was among his own racial group. This also highlights the benefit that students draw simply from attending college with a student population that is different from the type of peers with whom they grew up.

Beyond cognitive growth and an improved confidence, those who interact constructively with others with different background, values, and experiences can also expect to widen their perspectives, deepen their cross-cultural understanding and skills, and thereby improve their possibilities for postgraduation work and even their psychological well-being.

They can also expect higher moral development. Studies reviewed by Pascarella and Terenzini (1991) found that "exposure to divergent perspectives . . . and cognitive moral conflict (such as courses presenting material from different perspectives)" are important in developing moral values (p. 355). This entails, for example, helping others, which the authors cited by Bok (2006)[3] report being a consequence of interracial interaction.

Many authors talk about this civic mindedness: those interacting with diverse others tend to develop an outward looking and less self-centered mindset. In Astin, Astin, and Lindholm's (2011) words, students' interaction across racial lines has a positive effect on their "ethic of caring," ecumenical worldview, and charitable involvement (p. 147). Similar effects were found by Riutta and Teodorescu (2014), who report that freshmen reporting most "diversity interactions" also showed most growth in Socially Responsible Leadership, which measures such things as citizenship and students' commitment to working with others for common purpose.

In sum, when studying diversity, scholars in the last fifteen years have focused on the beneficial aspects of *positive* interactions between students and the consequences such interactions have for students' cognition and social skills, attitude toward multiculturalism, and propensity for civic action (Astin, 1993; Chang et al., 2004, 2006; Gurin et al., 2002; Hu & Kuh, 2003; Hurtado, 2005; Laird, 2005; Levin et al., 2003; Pascarella & Terenzini, 2005).

Yet not every interaction between diverse college students is positive. While what are called negative diversity interactions—interactions with diverse students[4] that are perceived as hurtful, hostile, and/or insulting—have received relatively little attention in scholarly research, the studies that do exist have found them to be consequential. For example, Hurtado (2005) found: "Negative interactions with diverse peers resulted in lower scores on many outcomes—including lower self-confidence in leadership, cultural awareness, concern for the public good . . . students' self-efficacy for social change, perspective taking . . . development of a pluralistic orientation . . . and the importance placed on making civic contributions" (p. 601).

Therefore, one will want to keep in mind that while students' exposure to discontinuity and conflict between their views and those of others can benefit them by challenging them to see issues from different perspectives, the potential for damaging negative interactions also exists. In their study of the freshman year in forty-seven institutions participating in the Wabash National Study, Riutta and Wen (2012) found that negative diversity interactions had a damaging effect on students' psychological well-being, intercultural effectiveness, and inclination for lifelong learning.

STUDENT AND FACULTY VIEWS AND BEST PRACTICES WITH DIVERSITY

Inclusivity

The most addressed theme among students when they were asked about their experiences with diversity and how a college should best navigate diversity questions was inclusivity. In contrast to exclusive diversity, which students defined simply as the presence on campus of various groups that do *not* really interact with each other, inclusive diversity is one in which there is "one big group of different people together," as one student put it. Another student echoed by saying inclusive diversity is a situation in which, "it's literally impossible for everybody to be in their own segregated groups." Yet a third one said, "Everyone is encouraged to participate in other cultures." In inclusive diversity, there is a campus-wide appreciation of differences.

International Students

In turn, faculty spoke a lot about how the increase in the share of international students on campus has affected their classrooms. Several of them have observed international students as having a higher work ethic. "International students have taken the classes more seriously," recounts a religion professor, continuing, "By and large, they have worked harder." English and physics professors affirmed, with the latter emphasizing that she finds her international students "exceptionally respectful and dedicated." She adds, "They take their education very seriously. In high school they teach physics more in other countries, so the international students come in better prepared. Some of them challenge me, and that is fine."

Several faculty also shared how international students bring diverse perspectives into class. In the words of a psychology professor, such diversity "expands the depth of learning in substantive ways." She gives a "beautiful example" from her class, in which a Chinese student said she does not understand the emphasis on children "in your country," explaining, "in China the emphasis is on the old." Such perspectives enhance the teaching of a subject and help students learn to think of issues from diverse perspectives.

Yet some faculty stressed that more benefits could be reaped from the additional perspectives that international students bring to class than are currently being reaped. For example, an English professor lamented that the campus has not tapped into the potential of international students. In the presence of a sizeable Chinese student body, she said, "there is some real opportunity to discuss work ethic, expectations for college, and, for example, Chinese politics. But we are not tapping into that."

She points out, "In our student body, one in every ten students is a mainland Chinese student, and we could learn a lot from them. We have an opportunity to educate ourselves about this country of which Americans know very little. Also, what is the impact that we can have on the Chinese students who will be going back to China?"

According to her, the views of the Chinese students would be especially beneficial in political science classes. "Chinese students are flocking into political science," she points out. "It is obvious why: they have never been able to talk about these things before." She hopes that faculty and students would talk about these issues in the classroom so all could really benefit not only from the different viewpoints but by learning what it is like to live in such a different political system.

How Diversity Affects Teaching

Regarding teaching diverse students, faculty also addressed some of the challenges in effectively capturing the interest and experiences of students from various nationalities and cultures with their subject matter and pedagogy. A religion professor said that while diverse perspectives in the classroom make the studying of religion easier (one can draw from the personal experiences related to the "plethora of traditions in the classroom"), he has not yet found a way to bring especially Chinese students' indifference to religion to the class.

In turn, a biology professor notes that particularly when discussing genetics and the issues of population growth, her international students have expressed different views to which she has not always felt adequately prepared to respond. "It becomes a challenge to temper some extreme views in a way that does not mislead the students," she says. Furthermore, a psychology professor has learned that not all of her analogies work in a diverse classroom.

There is also the question of whether other HIPs, particularly pedagogies based on active learning, work in a diverse context. Some interviewed faculty lamented the lack of active participation by many international students in their classes. A sociology professor shares how he has addressed it: "I stopped class early one day and asked these Asian kids to stay. They thought they were in trouble. I told them talking and asking questions in class in this culture is not something to be punished for. It is something for which you will be rewarded."

Other faculty emphasize that it is particularly the pedagogies of active learning that are *most* suitable in a diverse context. According to a professor of classical languages, "Any student-centered pedagogy can help a class succeed in the face of diversity. For example, having students discuss readings in class in groups assigned by the teacher can help to ensure that students in different peer groups will interact. Formalized debates are good too. Different students shine in different kinds of activities." He emphasizes that it is really important to use a variety of different sorts of student centered activities. "They work because a typical problem created by diversity is that only a few students talk, while others do not."

Another thing to keep in mind comes from another English professor who describes his literature class. In this class, with several international students, "you have to take more time with basic English language and cultural references." This echoes the point highlighted in Light's (2001) research about the importance of getting students to a place where they have adequately similar (language) skills for the learning opportunity to be meaningful to all. Yet the professor would not utilize the natural advantage that American students have in the literature class by having the American students teach what they think about the text being discussed to the international students: "I do not like the idea of having experts outside of the text."

There are also other perspectives, depending on the discipline. Teachers of some disciplines do not find there is a need to adjust teaching based on the presence of international students. For example, the professor of classical languages cited above has not found that the change in student demographics has had—and does not believe it will have—much of an impact on teaching foreign languages.

He explains:

> Conflicting statements have been made about language study and foreign students. Some say that languages should not be required of foreign students. Language teachers do not agree. The average grades of all foreign students in my classes have been higher than those of native students. International students are not harmed in their other classes by studying foreign languages—in fact, it can help their English comprehension. Also, they often have an advantage over American students in language classes. For example, in studying Ancient Greek and Latin, students who have already studied English as a foreign language have experience in second-language acquisition.

Based on his experience, neither are international students disadvantaged in his classical literature classes. The fact that in these classes, "the cultural context is never assumed benefits international students," he says. "These students often come to the study of foreign cultures more objectively, whereas some American students may think they know a lot about Caesar and Ancient Rome because they had a Latin class in high school, or that they understand the relevance of the Classics in our culture because they know about Caesar salad or Caesar's palace."

Thus the pedagogies that work and do not work in a diverse context vary by discipline and the particular dynamics and goals of each class. Common strategies the faculty use include trying to get students to draw from their own backgrounds, understanding both differences and commonalities between people, understanding the importance of individuals, not just group characteristics, and taking into account diverse learning styles.

In addition to pedagogical strategies, a diverse campus also needs to pay attention to students' interpersonal relations as the presence of large numbers of students whose backgrounds, values, and viewpoints differ significantly from each other also increases the likelihood of negative diversity interactions. We know that campus social environments and peer relationships, in particular, are "critically important for transition to college and academic success" (Locks et al., 2008, p. 264). Increasingly, students' relations with diverse peers form a major part of these peer relationships.

What does all this mean for the operation of HIPs? In the absence of student diversity, students would not be able to "hear" and "touch" diversity in the same way in the classroom, making internalizing and applying diverse perspectives more difficult. Also, it would seem that if students first cannot get along with each other, implementing other HIPs with success would be much harder. For one, students could not engage effectively in collaborative learning.

The challenge for colleges is how to foster constructive interactions and learning from diversity so that interactions in college have the desired effect of fostering further interactions, understanding, and good will, and helping develop both cognitive and social skills in students. This may call for faculty to incorporate more student-centered pedagogies and modify their lesson plans, and staff to revisit types and ways of student-life programming, but it seems that the gains are well worth the costs. With the increasingly diverse nation and workforce, the ability to relate to and understand diverse others seems a prerequisite for successful life beyond college.

NOTES

1. According to Pascarella, Edison, Nora, Hagedorn, & Terenzini (1996), by 2080 the United States will be less than 50 percent white.

2. Orfield, G., & Yun, J. T., (1999). *Resegregation in American schools*. Cambridge, MA: Civil Rights Project, Harvard University.

3. Gurin, P., Lehman, J. S., & Lewis, E. (2004). *Defending diversity: Defending affirmative action at the University of Michigan*. Ann Arbor: University of Michigan Press, pp. 102, 130.

4. Students from different racial, cultural, or religious backgrounds, or students with different values or political views.

EIGHT
Summary and Conclusions

This study began as an effort to better understand the evidence that we had, first anecdotally, and then objectively, of the unusual success of students in Emory's Oxford College across a broad range of learning and development outcomes. We wanted to understand teaching practices and in general the educational strategies employed by faculty and staff on this campus with higher-than-expected retention and graduation rates, high rates of majority- and minority-student degree completion in STEM fields, and students' above-average frequency of engagement in service and leadership activities.

In individual faculty interviews and student focus groups, we identified specific practices in frequent use across the campus that are identified in the higher-education literature as high-impact educational practices (HIPs). In reviewing the literature, it became evident that although HIPs are well known across the higher-education landscape, there are few if any published works on the perspectives and experiences of either faculty or students regarding on- or off-campus implementation of these practices. Intuitively, it is easy to think of what is meant by, for example, high-quality student–faculty interaction, but in practical terms, it is much harder to say how faculty can successfully promote such interaction.

In semistructured interviews, fifty-five faculty, staff/members of the administration, and students shared their views about "how students learn best" and what they thought about a number of specific HIPs. While most faculty, and especially students, did not use the phrase "high-impact practices" when describing effective teaching methods, their comments revealed that the benefits of HIPs as recognized by the higher-education community were the same as those reported by the faculty and students.

So while this study did not systematically examine learning outcomes, it was clear from student and faculty testimonies that learning increased and improved when HIPs were used. For example, when faculty described the assignments they had used that had "worked," producing learning, it was evident that such assignments had several characteristics of the HIPs.

FINDINGS

The discussion of HIPs started with high academic expectations and moved to more concrete actions and approaches—such as how faculty can help students navigate high expectations and interpersonal relationships while maintaining a balanced life in general. It described some of the ways those expectations are experienced by both students and faculty (for example, in student–faculty research). As the last chapter, the study placed all the HIPs in the context in which HIPs will be increasingly employed in the future, namely a high level of student diversity. An increasing share of college students will experience college—and HIPs—amid diverse college peers and surrounding community.

The first area to which the study sought to contribute concerned identifying campus environment, structure, and culture that are most conducive to the widespread and effective use of HIPs. Based on comments from both faculty and administrators, such an environment starts with institutional priorities and values centered on faculty teaching skills, innovation, and cooperation. Emphasis on teaching should be reflected in recruitment decisions and decisions about faculty promotion and tenure.

Consequently, related areas—such as how and to what extent student course evaluations are considered as part of promotion and tenure decisions—should reflect such institutional values. A logical approach is that course evaluations should be assessed primarily on the basis of the instructor's teaching effectiveness, improvement over time, and commitment to course development. The perfecting of all these takes time.

Institutional values should also be manifest in what is *not* expected of faculty—such as voluminous research production—if teaching is the focus of the institution. There should also be adequate support structures including at the departmental level and incentives to facilitate high-contact teaching and interaction with students. Faculty should be able to spend ample time with students, since a high level of contact is a key element of the HIPs.

One way that the emphasis on teaching and frequent contact with students can be supported is in a lighter course load and/or smaller section enrollments so that individual faculty can concentrate on work with fewer students. In Oxford College, for example, faculty teaching the physical sciences (with accompanying labs) teach a maximum of forty-eight students per semester. In the other disciplines, the number is also low at fifty to ninety per semester.

Student and faculty interviews also revealed that HIPs are easier to implement and learning is maximized when, in science classes, instructors teach their own laboratory sections. This means that faculty know, and work with, each student individually. Again, this requires that class size is kept small. At Oxford College, introductory science classes typically enroll a maximum of twenty-four students in both recitation and lab sessions.

Another part of the institutional structure and culture that encourages and strengthens the use of HIPs is a close cooperation between academic and co- or extracurricular life, especially with an emphasis on community engagement. These provide more opportunities and support for students to take what they learn in the classroom into the community, and vice versa, strengthening both the active learning component of classes and real-life application.

The second question this study addressed was whether freshman- and sophomore-level students were ready for HIPs. Faculty descriptions of their teaching experiences and student success and feedback indicated that the use of HIPs in freshman and sophomores years significantly enhances learning, and that freshmen are not too young to engage in even the HIPs that are typically thought of as more appropriate for later college years (e.g., undergraduate research). In fact, early exposure to them seems to boost success in later years.

Implementing HIPs during the freshman and sophomore years also means that HIPs support general education goals. This study's finding is that HIPs, such as setting of high expectations, research with faculty (including disciplinary research), and leadership experiences *can* be successfully employed in general education courses just as readily and with the same beneficial effects as in disciplinary courses supporting the major.

When students learn to conduct research early on, collaborate with and lead others, and work effectively in a diverse environment, they will be better equipped for their upper-level courses, in which they will need these same skills. Utilizing HIPs in general education courses could be conceived of as a tool to help jump start deeper learning (refer to Kuh [2008] about the higher level of [perceived] learning by those exposed to HIPs).

It is also the experience of Oxford College that the positive impact of HIPs is amplified when students engage in HIPs in a diverse context. A high degree of student diversity not only characterizes the contemporary context of the study institution but is expected to be characteristic of most college campuses in the future. Working collaboratively with peers from various countries, cultures, socioeconomic backgrounds, and religions requires students to develop interpersonal and social skills grounded in an awareness and sensitivity toward others in the classroom and throughout their time on campus.

The third focus of this study was to examine faculty strategies in each HIP. Faculty and student interviews revealed that each of the HIPs can be utilized across the disciplines, although some HIPs are more readily employed in some disciplines than others. For example, undergraduate research finds an easier fit in the natural sciences than in the humanities. Classroom diversity connects more easily with content in the humanities than in the natural sciences.

But overall, faculty strategies in employing HIPs are varied and applicable across the curriculum. These include, for example, integrating an element of surprise in the classroom to support active and student-centered learning, engaging students in the feedback process, and overall setting an expectation for students to be more responsible for their own learning.

Beyond faculty and student experiences with individual HIPs, there are a few broader conclusions that emerge from this study. First, founded on the combination of high academic expectations and support of students, a campus that demonstrates built-in redundancies and *repetition* of the HIPs in the classroom ensures that students have frequent exposure to them. Frequent experience of HIPs reinforces their beneficial impact. This means these practices should be present in strategies by individual faculty, leadership opportunities, and programs such as service learning.

Second, especially in inquiry-based classes, a HIP-rich approach to general education stimulates *student curiosity and questioning*. Undergraduate research, service learning, and peer-to-peer interaction within a diverse student body all incorporate elements of student surprise, exposure to contexts to which students are not used, and in general the utilization and expectation of active learning. Faculty used terminology like keeping students on their toes, keeping *themselves* on their toes, making unexpected ("diagonal") connections between topics and classes, and presenting information in a surprising context (such as in a prison).

Cultivation of students' curiosity is an integral part of "inquiry" classes. In the process of teaching these, faculty on the study campus have invested heavily in understanding the process of learning. So, while the inquiry classes emphasize disciplinary learning—that is, how knowledge is produced and processed in each field—they also underscore the general importance of learning, thinking, and evaluating knowledge apart from any particular discipline. In the words of a chemistry instructor, "Thinking is what we try to develop—not ability to follow cooking instructions."

In helping students learn to think, faculty integrate elements of surprise and change, and place the responsibility for learning with the students early on. The sequence in which challenge, curiosity, and engagement combine to produce learning is (1) a challenging assignment in which students must identify important questions, followed by (2) student engagement with those questions and the development of answers, and (3) students' reflection on their experiences with the assignment including reflection on their learning.

Third, the interviews uncovered a level of *respect and seriousness with which faculty regard their students,* revealed by the ways in which they spoke about their freshmen and sophomores. They explicitly emphasized that it is important to take students' ideas seriously and admit that faculty can learn from students. Science faculty emphasized the importance of sharing with students the excitement about research and joint research projects—not as equal peers but as partners. They spoke of the importance of thinking about and showing concern for students' future choices, life after college, and students as whole persons.

Finally, from the prevalence of HIPs on a campus, with multiple instances of HIPs across the curriculum, what emerges is an understanding that *the whole is greater than the sum of its parts.* As a group, HIPs have in common the fact that they either demand or provide important support for active learning. As students' encounters with HIPs become more frequent, there is a synergy among these encounters that builds students' capacity for active learning. At some point, students' experiences of HIPs will become so frequent that active learning will become the norm and students will take from the experience new habits of mind expected to last a lifetime.

FURTHER IMPLICATIONS FOR OTHER INSTITUTIONS

The study highlighted several times how a small campus can facilitate many of the HIPs in ways that would be much more difficult on a larger campus—for example, engaged and active learning is much easier to accomplish in small classes and on a campus in which faculty and students cross each other's paths frequently. On larger campuses, it is via learning communities in particular that such experiences could most practically be replicated. The effective size of the community does matter, as many of the students and faculty emphasized in their interviews.

In other institutions, the elements of student curiosity, questioning, and inquiry combined with challenge should be expected to produce the same kinds of results as on the study campus. On the study campus, across the pedagogies and programs, one very pronounced, recurring theme in faculty interviews was to begin with the mind of the student. Phrases like "student engagement" and "student inquiry" are abundant in the campus literature and in course syllabi. To begin with, the student may sound so obvious as to be self-evident, but the shift from the primacy of information to an emphasis on student inquiry, while subtle, is significant.

Students learn and integrate their learning best when they are more fully engaged by their own questions. The affective domain becomes involved, and personal motivation lends support to their efforts. When curiosity and question making are then joined with academic rigor and challenge, students are challenged to develop something that is fundamentally personal into a scholarly inquiry.

Also, taking students seriously and being intentional about respecting their minds can lead to success in such things as freshman facilitation of classroom discussion, freshman collaboration in research with faculty, and freshman leadership on campus. Also, using an interactive feedback process and giving room for student experiences in the classroom highlight the active role that students can play and respect their thoughts and experiences.

Finally, as suggested above, the clustering of HIPs, or integrating them in several classes as well as student life, creates the critical mass — exposure to HIPs throughout the campus experience. So, instead of developing one strong program, the effectiveness of HIPs is likely greater if they are integrated within the entire campus culture. This can be accomplished through a general education program that facilitates HIPs such as active and collaborative learning.

It is also vital to forge partnerships between student life and academic life, so that what happens in the classroom is reinforced outside of it. And furthermore, a campus-wide emphasis on student engagement, creative pedagogy, and faculty development are vital ingredients of successfully implementing HIPs. It is in such an environment in which general education programs and other programs directed at freshman and sophomore students can expect to maximize learning for the rest of the college years and beyond.

References

Agrell, J. (2007). The value of mistakes. *Horn Call, 37*(3), 55–56.

Alderman, R. V. (2008). *Faculty and student out-of-classroom interaction: Student perceptions of quality of interaction.* Doctoral dissertation. Texas A&M University.

Allport, G. A. (1954). *The nature of prejudice.* Cambridge, MA: Addison-Wesley.

American Psychological Association. (2011). The state of mental health of college campuses: A growing crisis. Retrieved from http://www.apa.org/about/gr/education/news/2011/college-campuses.aspx

Arum, R., & Roksa, J. (2011). *Academically adrift: Limited learning on college campuses.* Chicago, IL: University of Chicago Press.

Astin, A. (1993). Diversity and multiculturalism on the campus: How are students affected? *Change, 25*(2), 44–49.

Astin, A. W., Astin, H. S., & Lindholm, J. A. (2011). *Cultivating the spirit: How college can enhance students' inner lives.* San Francisco, CA: Jossey-Bass.

Ball State University Task Force on Academic Rigor. (2013). Academic rigor task force report. Retrieved from http://cms.bsu.edu/sitecore/shell//-/media/WWW/DepartmentalContent/Senate/Task%20Force%20on%20Academic%20Rigor/ARigor2013Final.pdf

Blanton, R. L. (2008). A brief history of undergraduate research, with consideration of its alternative futures. In R. Taraban, & R. L. Blanton, (Eds.), *Creating effective undergraduate research programs in science: The transformation from student to scientist* (pp. 233–46). New York, NY: Teachers College Press.

Bok, D. (2006). *Our underachieving colleges: A candid look at how much students learn and why they should be learning more.* Princeton, NJ: Princeton University Press.

Bonwell, C. C., & Eison, J. A. (1991). *Active learning: Creating excitement in the classroom.* ASHE-ERIC Higher Education Report No. 1. Washington, DC: The George Washington University, School of Education and Human Development.

Bowen, S. (1999). The Oxford College faculty. In S. Bowen, J. W. Wagner, & E. Lewis (Eds.), *The Oxford students* (pp. 5–7). White Paper. Oxford, GA: Oxford College of Emory University.

Boyer, E. L. (1987). *College: The undergraduate experience in America.* The Carnegie Foundation for the Advancement of Teaching. New York, NY: Harper & Row.

Braxton, J. M., ed. (2009). Understanding the development of the whole person. *Journal of College Student Development, 50*(6), 573–75.

Brownell, J. E., & Swaner, L. E. (2009a). High-impact practices: Applying the learning outcomes literature to the development of successful campus programs. *Peer Review*, Spring. Washington, DC: Association of American Colleges & Universities.

Brownell, J. E., & Swaner, L. E. (2009b). Outcomes of high-impact educational practices: A literature review. *Diversity & Democracy, 12*(2), 4–6. Washington, DC: Association of American Colleges & Universities.

California State University at Chico. (n.d.). Academic rigor at California State University, Chico. Retrieved from http://www.csuchico.edu/phil/shared/rigor.htm

Chang, M. J., Astin, A. W., & Kim, D. (2004). Cross-racial interaction among undergraduates: Some consequences, causes, and patterns. *Research in Higher Education, 45*(5), 529–52.

Chang, M. J., Denson, N., Saenz, V., & Misa, K. (2006). The educational benefits of sustaining cross-racial interaction among undergraduates. *The Journal of Higher Education, 77*(3), 430–55.

Chickering, A. W., & Gamson, Z. F. (1987). Seven principles for good practice in undergraduate education. *AAHE Bulletin*, March, 3–7. Washington, DC: American Association for Higher Education.

Densmore, K. (2000). Service learning and multicultural education: Suspect or transformative? In C. R. O'Grady, (Ed.), *Integrating service learning and multicultural education in colleges and universities*. Mahwah, NJ: Lawrence Erlbaum Associates.

Duke University. (n.d.). *Humanities writ large*. http://humanitieswritlarge.duke.edu/undergraduate-research

Eagan, K., Figueroa, T., Hurtado, S.,& Gasiewski, J. (2012). Faculty accessibility cues: Opening the doors for classroom communications. Presentation at the Association for Institutional Research (AIR) Annual Forum. New Orleans, LA. http://www.docstoc.com/docs/156870750/Faculty-Accessibility-Cues

Edwards, D. (2008). International engagements: The characteristics of international students' engagement with university. *AUSSE Research Briefings*, 2. July.

Fechheimer, M., Webber, K., & Kleiber, P. B. (2011). How well do undergraduate research programs promote engagement and success of students? *CBE—Life Sciences Education, 10*(2), 156–63. Retrieved from http://www.ncbi.nlm.nih.gov/pmc/articles/PMC3105922/

Finley, A. (2011). Assessment of high-impact practices: Using findings to drive change in the Compass Project. *Peer Review, 13*(2), 29–33. Washington, DC: Association of American Colleges and Universities.

Finley, A., & McNair, T. (2013). *Assessing underserved students' engagement in high-impact practices*. Washington, DC: Association of American Colleges and Universities.

Gamer, Brad. (2013). Pursuing academic rigor one course at a time. *The toolbox: A teaching and learning resource for instructors, 11*(6), 1–2. Retrieved from http://tech.sa.sc.edu/fye/toolbox/files/11_06.pdf

Gokhale, A. A. (1995). Collaborative learning enhances critical thinking. *Journal of Technology Education, 7*(1), 22–30.

Gurin, P., Dey, E. L., Hurtado, S., & Gurin, G. (2002). Diversity and higher education: Theory and impact on educational outcomes. *Harvard Educational Review, 72*(3), 330–66.

Gurung, R. A., Chick, N. L., & Haynie, A., (Eds.) (2008). *Exploring signature pedagogies: Approaches to teaching disciplinary habits of mind*. Sterling, VA: Stylus Publishing.

Hefling, K. (2013). Obama administration pushes colleges on diversity. *Huffington Post*, September 27. http://www.huffingtonpost.com/2013/09/27/obama-college-diversity_n_4000218.html

Hu, S., & Kuh, G. (2003). Diversity experiences and college student learning and personal development. *Journal of College Student Development, 44*(3), 320–34.

Hurley, D. J., Harnisch, T. L., Moran, R. L., & Parker, E. A. (2013). Top 10 higher education policy issues for 2013. A Higher Education Policy Brief. *AASCU Policy Matters*, January. Washington, DC: American Association of State Colleges and Universities.

Hurtado, S. (2005). The next generation of diversity and intergroup relations research. *Journal of Social Issues, 61*(3), 595–610.

Hurtado, S., Milem, J., Clayton-Pedersen, A., & Allen, W. (1999). Enacting diverse learning environments: Improving the climate for racial/ethnic diversity in higher education. *ERIC Digest*, ED430513 1999-00-00. Washington, DC: ERIC Clearinghouse on Higher Education, the George Washington University. In cooperation with the Association for the Study of Higher Education. http://files.eric.ed.gov/fulltext/ED430513.pdf

Jacoby, B. (1996). Service learning in today's higher education. In B. Jacoby, & Associates (Eds.), *Service-learning in higher education: Concepts and practices*. San Francisco, CA: Jossey-Bass.

Johnson, D. W., Johnson, R. T., & Smith, K. A. (1991). *Cooperative learning: Increasing college faculty instructional productivity*. ASHE-ERIC Higher Education Report No. 4.

Washington, DC: The George Washington University, School of Education and Human Development.

Jones, T. W. (2005). The realities of diversity and the campus climate for first-year students. In M. L. Upcraft, J. N. Gardner, & B. O. Barefoot, (Eds.), *Challenging and supporting the first-year student: A handbook for improving the first year of college*. San Francisco, CA: Jossey-Bass.

Kendall, J. C., & Associates. (1990). *Combining service and learning: A resource book for community and public service*. Raleigh, NC: National Society for Internships and Experiential Education.

King, P. M., Baxter Magolda, M. B., & Massé, J. C. (2011). Maximizing learning from engaging across difference: The role of anxiety and meaning making. *Equity & Excellence in Education, 44*(4), 468–87.

Knapper, C. K. (Ed.) (2007). *Experiences with inquiry learning*. Hamilton: Centre for Leadership in Learning, McMaster University.

Kuh, G. D. (2008). *High-impact educational practices: What they are, who has access to them, and why they matter*. Washington, DC: Association of American Colleges and Universities.

Kuh, G., Kinzie, J., Schuh, J. H., & Whitt, E. J. (2005). *Student success in college: Creating conditions that matter*. San Francisco, CA: Jossey-Bass.

Laird, T. F. N. (2005). College students' experiences with diversity and their effects on academic self-confidence, social agency, and disposition toward critical thinking. *Research in Higher Education, 46*(4), 365–87.

Langseth, M. (2000). Maximizing impact, minimizing harm: Why service-learning must more fully integrate multicultural education. In C. R. O'Grady, (Ed.), *Integrating service learning and multicultural education in colleges and universities*. Mahwah, NJ: Lawrence Erlbaum Associates.

Lee, V. S. (Ed.) (2004). *Teaching and learning through inquiry: A guidebook for institutions and instructors*. Sterling, VA: Stylus Publishing.

Lee, V. S. (2012). What is inquiry-guided learning? In V. Lee (Ed.), Inquiry-Guided Learning. *New Directions for Teaching and Learning, 129*, 5–14.

Levin, S., van Laar, C., & Sidanus, J. (2003). The effects of ingroup and outgroup friendships on ethnic attitudes in college: A longitudinal study. *Group Processes & Intergroup Relations, 6*(1), 76–92.

Light, R. J. (2001). *Making the most of college: Students speak their minds*. Cambridge, MA: Harvard University Press.

Locks, A. M., Hurtado, S., Bowman, N. A., & Oseguera, L. (2008). Extending notions of campus climate and diversity to students' transition to college. *The Review of Higher Education, 31*(3), 257–85.

Marcus, J. M., Hughes, T. M., McElroy, D. M., & Wyatt, R. E. (2010). Engaging first-year undergraduates in hands-on research experiences: The upper green river barcode of life project. *Journal of College Science Teaching*, January/February, 39–45. Retrieved from http://www.uky.edu/academy/sites/www.uky.edu.academy/files/Engaging%20First-Year%20Undergraduates.pdf

Mayhew, M. J., Seifert, T. A., & Pascarella, E. (2012). How the first year of college influences moral reasoning development for students in moral consolidation and moral transition. *Journal of College Student Development, 53*(1), 19–40.

Mazur, E. (2013). Enhancing learning through peer instruction. Presentation. Institute for the Pedagogy in the Liberal Arts. Oxford, GA: Oxford College of Emory University.

McNair, T., & Albertine, S. (2012). Seeking high-quality, high-impact learning: The imperative of faculty development and curricular intentionality. *Peer Review, 14*(3), 4–5. Washington, DC: Association of American Colleges and Universities.

Miami University-Ohio. (n.d.). Miami Undergraduate Research. Retrieved from https://www.muohio.edu/research/undergraduate/index.html

Millis, B. J. (2002) Enhancing learning—and more!—through cooperative learning. IDEA Paper #38. The IDEA Center. Retrieved from http://www.theideacenter.org/sites/default/files/IDEA_Paper_38.pdf

Millis, B. J. (2010). Why faculty should adopt cooperative learning approaches. In B. J. Millis (Ed.), *Cooperative learning in higher education: Across the disciplines, across the academy* (pp. 1–10). Sterling, VA: Stylus.

Millis, B. J. (2012). Active learning strategies in face-to-face courses. IDEA Paper #53. Manhattan, KS: The IDEA Center.

Moon, J. (2009). Community engagement and leadership. In S. Bowen, J. W. Wagner, & E. Lewis (Eds.), *The Oxford students* (pp. 22–25). White Paper. Oxford, GA: Oxford College of Emory University.

Nepo, Mark. (2010). Foreword. In Palmer, P. J., & Zajonc, A. (with Schribner, M.), *The heart of higher education: Transforming the academy through collegial conversations*. San Francisco, CA: Jossey-Bass.

O'Grady, C. R. (Ed.). (2000). *Integrating service learning and multicultural education in colleges and universities*. Mahwah, NJ: Lawrence Erlbaum Associates.

Oxford College of Emory University. (n.d.). INQ Faculty Development Wiki. Available at http://oxmedia.oxford.emory.edu/wiki/index.php/Main_Page

Ozturk, M., & Debelak, C. (n.d.). Setting realistically high academic standards and expectations. http://www.usca.edu/essays/vol152005/ozturkrev.pdf

Pakala, K., & Haight, S. (2010). Supporting student success with time-efficient faculty-student interactions. PowerPoint slides. http://stem.boisestate.edu/wp-content/uploads/2013/03/CTL_FSI_Krishna_Sarah_Mar155.pdf

Palmer, P. J., and Zajonc, A. (with Schribner, M.) (2010). *The heart of higher education: Transforming the academy through collegial conversations*. San Francisco, CA: Jossey-Bass.

Panitz, Theodore. (1999). Collaborative versus cooperative learning: A comparison of the two concepts which will help us understand the underlying nature of interactive learning. Opinion paper. http://files.eric.ed.gov/fulltext/ED448443.pdf

Pascarella, E. T., & Terenzini, P. T. (1991). *How college affects students: Findings and insights from twenty years of research*. The Jossey-Bass Higher and Adult Education Series. San Francisco, CA: Jossey-Bass.

Pascarella, E. T., & Terenzini, P. T. (2005). *How college affects students: A third decade of research*. Vol. 2. San Francisco, CA: Jossey-Bass.

Pascarella, E. T., Edison, M., Nora, A., Hagedorn, L. S., & Terenzini, P. T. (1996). Influences on students' openness to diversity and challenge in the first year of college. *The Journal of Higher Education, 67*(2), 174–95.

Paulson, D. R., & Faust, J. L. (n.d.) Active learning for the college classroom. Resource page. California State University. Retrieved from http://www.calstatela.edu/dept/chem/chem2/Active/#group

Putnam, R. D. (1993). *Making democracy work: Civic traditions in modern Italy*. Princeton, NJ: Princeton University Press.

Putnam, R. D. (1995). Bowling alone: America's declining social capital. *Journal of Democracy, 6*(1), 65–78.

Putnam, R. D. *Bowling alone: The collapse and revival of American community*. New York, NY: Simon & Schuster.

Quinlan, K. M. (2011). *Developing the whole student: Leading higher education initiatives that integrate mind and heart*. Stimulus paper. University of Oxford: Oxford Learning Institute. Retrieved from http://www.learning.ox.ac.uk/media/global/wwwadminoxacuk/localsites/oxfordlearninginstitute/documents/overview/research/publications/Quinlan_Developing_2011.pdf

Riutta, S., & Teodorescu, D. (2014). Leadership development on a diverse campus. *Journal of College Student Development, 55*(8), 830–36.

Riutta, S., & Wen, H-M. (2012). Understanding and minimizing negative interactions among diverse peers using Wabash National Study of Liberal Arts Education data.

Presentation at the Southern Association for Institutional Research Annual Conference, September 22–25. Orlando, FL.

Rosenberger, C. (2000). Beyond empathy: Developing critical consciousness through service learning. In C. R. O'Grady (Ed.), *Integrating service learning and multicultural education in colleges and universities*. Mahwah, NJ: Lawrence Erlbaum Associates.

Schaller, M. A. (2005). Wandering and wondering: Traversing the uneven terrain of the second college year. *About Campus*, July-August, 17–24.

Schantz, M. S. (2008). Undergraduate research in the humanities: Challenges and prospects. *Council on Undergraduate Research (CUR) Quarterly*, 29(2), 26–29.

Schilling, K. M., & Schilling, K. L. (1999). Increasing expectations for student effort. *About Campus*, May-June, 4–10.

Shadle, S. E. (2010). Cooperative learning in general chemistry through process-oriented guided inquiry learning. In B. J. Millis (Ed.), *Cooperative learning in higher education: Across the disciplines, across the academy* (pp. 35–56). Sterling, VA: Stylus.

Shulman, L. S. (2005). Signature pedagogies in the professions. *Dædalus*, Summer. American Academy of Arts & Sciences.

Smith-Barrow, D. (2014). Universities that attract the most international students. February 11. Retrieved from http://www.usnews.com/education/best-colleges/the-short-list-college/articles/2013/05/07/universities-that-draw-the-most-international-students

Song, J. (2014). Obama encourages economic diversity in higher education. *Los Angeles Times*, January 17. Retrieved from http://www.latimes.com/local/la-me-obama-college-20140117,0,5349627.story#axzz2qi62ZcSN

Stephan, W. G., & Finlay, K. (1999). The role of empathy in improving intergroup relations. *Journal of Social Issues*, 55(4), 729–43.

Tagg, J. (2003). *The learning paradigm college*. Bolton, MA: Anker Publishing Company, Inc.

Tanner, K. & Allen, D. (2005). Approaches to biology teaching and learning: Understanding the wrong answers—teaching toward conceptual change. *Cell Biology Education*, 4(2): 112–17.

The Boyer Commission on Educating Undergraduates in the Research University. (1998). *Reinventing undergraduate education: A blueprint for America's research universities*. Sponsored by Carnegie Foundation for the Advancement of Teaching, Princeton, NJ. Stony Brook, NY.

Uhl, C. (with Stuchul, D. L.) (2011). *Teaching as if life matters: The promise of a new education culture*. Baltimore, MD: Johns Hopkins University Press.

University of Wisconsin-Madison. (n.d.). Undergraduate research scholars program. Retrieved from http://urs.ls.wisc.edu/.

Wabash National Study of Liberal Arts Institution. (n.d.). Effective teaching practices and institutional conditions from the Wabash National Study. Retrieved from http://web.uri.edu/assessment/files/WabashGoodPractices.pdf

Wabash National Study of Liberal Arts Institution. (2006–2012.) Overview of the study available at http://www.liberalarts.wabash.edu/study-overview/.

Wiggins, G. P., & McTighe, J. (2005). *Understanding by design*. Alexandria, VA: Association for Supervision and Curriculum Development (ASCD).

Zlotkowski, E. (Ed.). (1998). *Successful service-learning programs: New models of excellence in higher education*. Bolton, MA: Anker Publishing Company, Inc.

Zlotkowski, E. (2005). Service-learning and the first-year student. In M. L. Upcraft, J. N. Gardner, & B. O. Barefoot, (Eds.), *Challenging and supporting the first-year student: A handbook for improving the first year of college*. San Francisco, CA: Jossey-Bass.

About the Authors

Dr. Satu Rogers recently concluded six and a half years leading the Office of Institutional Research at Oxford College of Emory University. With a lead role in assessment of student learning and educational research, she advised and assisted Oxford College faculty in the design and conduct of research on teaching and learning. Prior to that, she studied the impact of civic education on citizen participation in Africa, publishing a research monograph, *Democratic Participation in Rural Tanzania and Zambia: The Impact of Civic Education* (2009). She has also published in the *Journal of College Student Development* and *Government and Opposition*. Rogers has given multiple research presentations in national conferences about student learning, particularly on the development of leadership skills and students' diversity interactions. At Oxford College, she also taught a qualitative research seminar about how to conduct research on student experiences with high-impact educational practices.

Dr. Jeffery Galle is Associate Professor of English and Director of the Center for Academic Excellence at Oxford College of Emory University. He has a long track record in pedagogy and faculty development. In the mid-90s, he served as Freshman Writing Director at a Louisiana university and coauthored a textbook, *Models for Composition*. He has led university workshops on teaching excellence as Outstanding Professor for the College of Arts and Sciences (University of Louisiana at Monroe, 2005), the Scott Professor for Teaching Excellence (ULM, 1996–1999), and as Distinguished Teaching Scholar (Emory University, 2009). Galle's recent publications on teaching, pedagogy, and faculty development have appeared in *The Teaching Professor, Teaching Theology and Religion, The International Journal for the Scholarship of Teaching & Learning*, and the *Louisiana English Journal*. In the past five years, he has presented more than a dozen papers and served on a number of academic panels at Association of American Colleges and Universities (AAC&U), Association for General and Liberal Studies (AGLS), and Association for Core Texts and Courses (ACTC). He currently serves as a consulting editor for the journal *College Teaching*, and his most recent publication on pedagogy is a coauthored chapter in *Inquiry-Based Learning for Faculty and Institutional Development: A Conceptual and Practical Resource for Educators* (Eds. P. Blessinger and J. M. Carfora, December 2014).